Learning
Elasticsearch 7.x

Index, Analyze, Search and
Aggregate Your Data Using Elasticsearch

Anurag Srivastava

www.bpbonline.com

FIRST EDITION 2021

Copyright © BPB Publications, India

ISBN: 978-93-89898-309

LIMITS OF LIABILITY AND DISCLAIMER OF WARRANTY

Distributors:

BPB PUBLICATIONS
20, Ansari Road, Darya Ganj
New Delhi-110002
Ph: 23254990/23254991

DECCAN AGENCIES
4-3-329, Bank Street,
Hyderabad-500195
Ph: 24756967/24756400

MICRO MEDIA
Shop No. 5, Mahendra Chambers,
150 DN Rd. Next to Capital Cinema,
V.T. (C.S.T.) Station, MUMBAI-400 001
Ph: 22078296/22078297

BPB BOOK CENTRE
376 Old Lajpat Rai Market,
Delhi-110006
Ph: 23861747

To View Complete
BPB Publications Catalogue
Scan the QR Code:

Published by Manish Jain for BPB Publications, 20 Ansari Road, Darya Ganj, New Delhi-110002 and Printed by him at Repro India Ltd, Mumbai

Dedicated to

My beloved parents
Shri Virendra Nath Srivastava
Shrimati Kiran Srivastava
&
My wife Chanchal and son Anvit

About the Author

Anurag Srivastava is works as Deputy Manager in the R&D centre of an air conditioning company. He has over 14 years of experience in the software industry and has led and handled teams and clients for more than 7 years. He is proficient in designing and deploying scalable applications and has multiple certifications in ML and data science using Python. He is well experienced with the Elastic stack (Elasticsearch, Logstash, and Kibana) for creating dashboards using system metrics data, log data, application data, or relational databases. Plus, he has good experience in some CI/CD and monitoring tools, like Jenkins, SonarQube, Graylog, and Kibana.

About the Reviewer

Pankaj has over 7 years of experience of working on front-end technologies like Angular, React, and EmberJS and currently works at Deskera as a senior software engineer. His skills in Angular and web application development, and more, have seen him become a Microsoft MVP and Google developer expert. Pankaj loves to share his knowledge with the community by speaking at various technical events and conferences. He is also the top contributor on stack overflow in India, and he ranks among the top 20 contributors in the world on Angular and AngularJS. He is also a technical reviewer for BPB Publication. He now focuses on channeling his knowledge into open-source projects and sharing it with the community by mentoring, creating POCS, running workshops, and writing blogs to help boost development in the world.

Acknowledgement

There are a few people I want to thank for their continued and ongoing support during the writing of this book. First and foremost, I would like to thank my wife for continuously encouraging me to write the book —I could have never completed it without her support.

I would also like to mention my parents, who have always supported me with all my assignments and trusted me throughout, giving me the confidence to complete this book.

My gratitude also goes to the team at BPB Publication for being supportive enough to provide me enough time to finish the book. They have supported me by providing me with feedback and incorporating my inputs.

Preface

This book is for developers, architects, DBA, DevOps, and other readers who want to learn Elasticsearch efficiently and apply it in their new/existing application. It is also beneficial to those who want to play with their data using Elasticsearch.

Basic computer programming is a perquisite, but no prior knowledge of Elasticsearch is required. required before starting this book as in this book we have covered Elasticsearch along with an introduction to other tools of Elastic Stack.

No prior knowledge of Elasticsearch is required before starting this book as this book starts from very basic and then goes to a very advanced topic gradually and practically through which anyone can easily understand the concepts.

This book has eleven chapters, in which you will learn the following:

Chapter 1 provides an overview of Elasticsearch and its components like cluster, nodes, index, document, and shard, and it also provides different use cases of Elasticsearch.

Chapter 2 covers the installation process of Elasticsearch. Here, we will talk about what's new in Elasticsearch 7.x, and then we will look at Elasticsearch installation on Linux using RPM, Debian package, macOS, and Windows.

Chapter 3 provides an introduction to Elastic Stack, where we will learn about Beats, Logstash, and Kibana. We will talk about the different components of Elastic Stack, that is, Elasticsearch, Logstash, Kibana, Beats, and such. We will also explain how each component works.

Chapter 4 looks at how to prepare the data before indexing. Here, we will cover different types of analyzers, normalizers, tokenizers, token filters and, character filters in Elasticsearch. We will also explain why it is important to prepare the data before indexing.

Chapter 5 walks you through how to import data from different sources into Elasticsearch. We will also discuss why data is so important for businesses and explain how to import data into Elasticsearch using different Beats and from different sources using Logstash.

Chapter 6 is about Elasticsearch index management. It explains how to create index, along with mapping. We will also perform index level operations and look at index APIs and the index life-cycle management.

Chapter 7 helps you understand the different search queries and how to construct the query for different use cases. We will cover the URI search and request body searches. We will also cover different APIs like multi search API, explain API, and profile API.

Chapter 8 explains how we can play around with Geodata and how to create queries and search based on distance. Here, we will understand the Geodata type and how to save Geo Point data and Geo Shape data. We will also see how to perform the Geo query by taking a practical use case.

Chapter 9 starts with an introduction to Elasticsearch aggregation and then looks at the different types of aggregation in Elasticsearch and how and when to aggregate data. We will also explain different types of aggregations like metrics aggregations, bucket aggregations, pipeline aggregations, and matrix aggregations.

Chapter 10 looks into performance tweaking, where we will check query profiling, cluster tuning, and other aspects of performance. We will explain how to tune Elasticsearch indexing speed, search speed, disk usage, and such. We will also understand Elasticsearch best practices to improve performance.

Chapter 11 covers Elasticsearch administration, like backup and restoration of Elasticsearch clusters, adding security, and creating index aliases. We will look at how to apply security on the Elasticsearch cluster, create index aliases, and such.

Errata

We take immense pride in our work at BPB Publications and follow best practices to ensure the accuracy of our content to provide with an indulging reading experience to our subscribers. Our readers are our mirrors, and we use their inputs to reflect and improve upon human errors, if any, that may have occurred during the publishing processes involved. To let us maintain the quality and help us reach out to any readers who might be having difficulties due to any unforeseen errors, please write to us at :

errata@bpbonline.com

Your support, suggestions and feedbacks are highly appreciated by the BPB Publications' Family.

Did you know that BPB offers eBook versions of every book published, with PDF and ePub files available? You can upgrade to the eBook version at www.bpbonline.com and as a print book customer, you are entitled to a discount on the eBook copy. Get in touch with us at :

business@bpbonline.com for more details.

At **www.bpbonline.com**, you can also read a collection of free technical articles, sign up for a range of free newsletters, and receive exclusive discounts and offers on BPB books and eBooks.

BPB is searching for authors like you

If you're interested in becoming an author for BPB, please visit **www.bpbonline.com** and apply today. We have worked with thousands of developers and tech professionals, just like you, to help them share their insight with the global tech community. You can make a general application, apply for a specific hot topic that we are recruiting an author for, or submit your own idea.

The code bundle for the book is also hosted on GitHub at **https://github.com/bpbpublications/Learning-Elasticsearch-7.x**. In case there's an update to the code, it will be updated on the existing GitHub repository.

We also have other code bundles from our rich catalog of books and videos available at **https://github.com/bpbpublications**. Check them out!

PIRACY

If you come across any illegal copies of our works in any form on the internet, we would be grateful if you would provide us with the location address or website name. Please contact us at **business@bpbonline.com** with a link to the material.

If you are interested in becoming an author

If there is a topic that you have expertise in, and you are interested in either writing or contributing to a book, please visit **www.bpbonline.com**.

REVIEWS

Please leave a review. Once you have read and used this book, why not leave a review on the site that you purchased it from? Potential readers can then see and use your unbiased opinion to make purchase decisions, we at BPB can understand what you think about our products, and our authors can see your feedback on their book. Thank you!

For more information about BPB, please visit **www.bpbonline.com**.

Table of Contents

CHAPTER 1
Getting Started with Elasticsearch

Introduction

This chapter provides an introduction to Elasticsearch, and we will start with the benefit of using Elasticsearch. We will then explain what Elasticsearch is, and you will get to know more about Elasticsearch and how it is built on top of Lucene is. After an introduction to Elasticsearch, we will cover its basic concepts by explaining the node, cluster, documents, index, and shards. Then, we will discuss the use cases of Elasticsearch like data search, data logging and analysis, application performance monitoring, system performance monitoring, data visualization, and so on. We will also cover various Elasticsearch clients that can be used with different languages like Java, PHP, Perl, Python, .NET, JavaScript, and such. At last, we will discuss how to use Elasticsearch as a primary data source, secondary data source, and as a standalone system.

Structure

In this chapter, we will discuss the following topics:

- What is Elasticsearch?
- The basic concepts of Elasticsearch
- Use cases of Elasticsearch
- Different clients for Elasticsearch

- How to use Elasticsearch

Objectives

After studying this unit, you should be able to:

- Understand the concepts of Elasticsearch
- Know how to use different Elasticsearch clients

Introduction to Elasticsearch

Elasticsearch exists to meet the need for a search mechanism to search the relevant data from a data store. However, before we jump to Elasticsearch, we should understand why search is so important. We are living in an information age where data is growing at an exponential rate due to digitization. There are several new data sources, such as smartwatches, smart devices, IoT sensors, online transactions, and many others, that generate data. This data can be structured or unstructured, it can be device-specific, or it can be time-series data. Data can be from different sources, and it can be of different types, so the first challenge is to streamline it by converting unstructured data into a structured form.

Ideally, these are the challenges we will face during data storage, but what would happen once the data is stored? If you want to find specific details in a hige dataset, it is going to be a challenging task without a search engine. Until some years ago, we were using RDBMS for all-purpose data storage, and the search operation was performed on the same RDBMS. Text search on the RDBMS system is a very difficult task, as we must write a complex SQL query that takes a lot of time even after applying all required indexes. Also, there are several other drawbacks like search relevancy, data aggregation, and so on, which exist in a search engine like Elasticsearch but not in an RDBMS system.

Search is important as we want to find exactly what we are looking for. For example, I want the topic of my interest from a blog site, so it must have a search mechanism to provide me the desired results quickly. Similarly, we need a quick search to get the desired products during online shopping sessions. It is very important to provide a quick search response with relevancy; otherwise, users will not use the application.

The search also has other aspects that we must consider:

- When I start searching, I should not have to type the complete word; the application should suggest the words as soon as I start typing.

- If I type the word wrong, the application should still suggest the products by applying the fuzzy data search.

- It should provide the feature of derivative search, where I can type the text, and it should match with any derivative of the text. For example, if I search for mobile, it should search for mobiles, phone/s, and such.

- It should support data aggregation so that we can show the user additional options with the search results. For example, if I search for mobile, it should provide me with filters like price range, ratings, brands, and so on, along with the count of the product in that range.

- It should provide relevant results; for example, if I am searching for a mobile phone, the application should first suggest the mobile phone and then its accessories, such as chargers, covers, headphones, and so on.

- It should be able to provide additional filters when I search for anything. For example, if I want a full HD screen resolution, 12 GB of RAM, and a specific color in my mobile search, the application should provide me with the results based on my filter.

- It should provide the search results within seconds so that users can get their products as soon as they hit the search button. If the search is taking minutes, we will lose the battle.

These are some of the core features of a search application that cannot be built using an RDBMS system. This system is good for data storage, but we should use alternate solutions along with the RDBMS for data search. Now that we have discussed the features that a search application should provide, let's discuss Elasticsearch. In the next section, we will see what Elasticsearch is and how it will solve these search-related issues.

What is Elasticsearch

Elasticsearch is an open-source search engine written in Java and built on top of Lucene. Lucene is a fast and high-performance search engine library that empowers the searching of Elasticsearch. We index the data to get the search results quickly, and the index can be of different types. Lucene uses an inverted index, wherein data structure is created to keep a list of each word. Now, you must be thinking why we should use Elasticsearch if Lucene provides everything. The answer is that Lucene is not easy to use directly because we need to write Java code to use it. Also, it is not distributed in nature, so it is not easy to expand it on multiple nodes. Elasticsearch uses the search feature of Lucene plus other extensions, which makes it the most famous search engine of the current time. It encapsulates the complexities of Lucene and provides REST APIs, using which we can easily interact with Elasticsearch. It also provides support for different programming languages through the language client, so we can code in any specific language and interact with Elasticsearch. We can also use the console to interact with Elasticsearch using CURL.

Elasticsearch was created by a company Elastic founded by Shay Banon, who has created it on top of Lucene. To summarize, Elasticsearch is an open-source, distributed, scalable, REST-based, document-oriented search engine built on top of Lucene. An Elasticsearch cluster can be run on a single server or hundreds of servers and can handle petabytes of data without any issue.

The basic concepts of Elasticsearch

It is important to understand a few terms that are used with Elasticsearch, such as cluster, node, index, document, and shards. We talk about these terminologies several times, so it is necessary to discuss them in brief here. We will discuss them in detail later.

Node

A node is a single running instance of Elasticsearch. Let's say we have an Elasticsearch cluster running on ten different servers; then, each server is known as a node. If we are not running the Elasticsearch on a production environment, we can run a single node cluster of Elasticsearch for some use cases, and we can call such nodes as a single node cluster of Elasticsearch. If the data size increases, we need more than one node to scale horizontally, which also provides fault tolerance to the solution. A node can transfer the client request to the appropriate node, as each node knows about the other ones in the cluster. Nodes can be of different types, which we will look at in the further sub-sections.

Master node

The master node is used for supervision as it tracks which node is part of the cluster or which shards to allocate to which nodes. The master node is important to maintain a healthy cluster of Elasticsearch. We can configure a master node by changing a node's `node.master` option as true in the Elasticsearch configuration file. If we want to create a dedicated master node, we must set other types as false in the configuration. Take a look at the following code:

```
node.master:            true
node.voting_only:       false
node.data:              false
node.ingest:            false
node.ml:                false
xpack.ml.enabled:       true
cluster.remote.connect: false
```

Here, you can see the `voting_only` option; if we set it false, the node will work as the master eligible node and can be picked as a master node. However, if we set the `voting_only` option as true, the node can participate in master node selection but cannot become a master node by itself. I will explain how master node selection works later.

Data node

Data nodes are responsible for storing data and performing CRUD operations on it. It also performs data search and aggregations. We can configure a data node by changing a node's `node.data` option to true in the Elasticsearch configuration file. If we want to create a dedicated data node, we must set other types as false in the configuration. Refer to the following code:

```
node.master:            false
node.voting_only:       false
node.data:              true
node.ingest:            false
node.ml:                false
cluster.remote.connect: false
```

Here, we are setting the `node.data` to true and all other options to false.

Ingest node

Ingest nodes are used to enrich and transform data before indexing it. So, they create an ingest pipeline using which data is transformed before indexing. We can configure an ingest node by changing a node's `node.ingest` option to true in the Elasticsearch configuration file. Any node can work as an ingest node, but if we have heavy data that we want to ingest, it is recommended to use a dedicated ingest node. To create a dedicated ingest node, we must set other types as false in the configuration. Refer to the following code:

```
node.master:            false
node.voting_only:       false
node.data:              false
node.ingest:            true
node.ml:                false
cluster.remote.connect: false
```

Here, we are setting the `node.ingest` to true and all other options to false.

Machine learning node

Elastic machine learning is not freely available, so if `xpack.ml.enabled` is set to true, we can create a machine learning node by changing the `node.ml` option to true. If we want to run machine learning jobs, we must change at least one node in the cluster as a machine learning node. To create a dedicated machine learning node, we must set other types as false in the configuration. Here's the code:

```
node.master:              false
node.voting_only:         false
node.data:                false
node.ingest:              false
node.ml:                  true
xpack.ml.enabled:         true
cluster.remote.connect:   false
```

So, we can change the node type to any of the preceding options, but a node has all the types by default.

Cluster

An Elasticsearch cluster consists of a set of one or many Elasticsearch nodes that work together. The distributed behavior of Elasticsearch allows us to scale it horizontally to different nodes that work together and form an Elasticsearch cluster. There are several advantages of the multi-node Elasticsearch cluster—it is fault-tolerant, which means we can run the cluster successfully even if some nodes fail. Also, we can accommodate huge data that cannot be stored on a single node (server). Elasticsearch cluster is smooth and easy to configure, and we can start with a single node cluster and can easily move to multi-node cluster setup by adding nodes.

Documents

An Elasticsearch document is a single record stored as a JSON document in a key-value pair, where the key is the name of the field, and the value is the value of that particular field. We store each record as a row in an RDBMS table, and Elasticsearch stores them as a JSON document. Elasticsearch documents are flexible, and we can store a different set of fields in each document. There is no limitation to store a fixed set of fields in each document of an index in Elasticsearch, unlike RDBMS tables, wherein we must fix the fields before inserting data.

Index

Elasticsearch index is a logical namespace to store similar types of documents. For example, we should create an index with the product name and start pushing the documents into the index if we want to store product details, as we have already discussed that Elasticsearch is built on top of Lucene and uses Lucene to write and read data from the index. An Elasticsearch index can be built of more than one Lucene index, and Elasticsearch does that using shards. Now, let's see what a shard is.

Shard

The distributed architecture of Elasticsearch is only possible due to shards. A shard is an independent and fully-functional Lucene index. A single Elasticsearch index can be split into multiple Lucene indices, which is why we can store huge data that cannot be stored on a single Elasticsearch node. Data can be split into multiple shards, and they can evenly be distributed to multiple nodes on the Elasticsearch cluster.

For example, if we have 100GB of data that we want to index and configured four shards, the 100GB data would be split into 25GB shards. If we have a single node, all four shards will stay on that node. If we add one more node to the cluster, the shards will evenly distribute on both. So, two shards will remain in node 1 while 2 will move to the second node of the cluster.

Shards can be of two types: primary and replica. Primary shards contain primary data, while replica shards contain a copy of the primary shards. We use the replica shards to protect us from any hardware failure and increase the search performance of the cluster.

The following image illustrates an Elasticsearch cluster with three nodes. It has the following shard configuration:

- Number of primary shards: 2
- Count of replica shards: 1

Now, if we have two nodes in the cluster—one primary and one replica—two shards will move to one node, while a primary two and replica one will move to the other node.

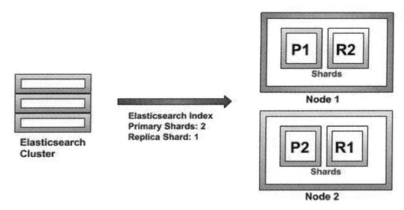

Figure 1.1: Elasticsearch shards

The preceding image shows the cluster with node 1 and node 2. On node 1, we have **P1** and **R2**, while we have the **P2** and **R1** shards on node 2. P denotes primary shards, and R denotes replica shards.

Use cases of Elasticsearch

We have already discussed some Elasticsearch features like analytics that can slice and dice the data so that we can get a complete insight. Analysis allows us to search even if the exact word is not matching or get search results even if someone types a wrong word using a fuzzy search. So, several Elasticsearch features are useful for many use cases. Although we cannot list all Elasticsearch use cases, the following are the main use cases.

Data search

The primary Elasticsearch use case is the data search, especially if the data size is huge. A decade ago, we were primarily using the RDBMS for data storage and search. Still, if we talk about the current situation, RDBMS is unable to perform well for data search as they are not built to perform a search engine operation. Elasticsearch is a search engine that is highly scalable and can provide quick results, along with features like aggregations, analysis, and fuzzy search, which makes it best for any data search-related use cases. The major domains that depend on Elasticsearch for data search are ecommerce portals, travel websites, social network websites, bioinformatics websites, news and blog portals, and such. They all need to show quick search results to win the battle with their competitors, as they lose cutomers if there is any delay in the search results. This is the primary Elasticsearch use case, wherein many companies are using its search feature.

Data logging and analysis

Data logging and analysis is another important area where we use Elasticsearch widely, along with other tools of the Elastic Stack like Beats, Logstash, and Kibana. Here, Beats and Logstash work as a data ingestion tool, using which we fetch data from different sources, such as log files, and push the data into Elasticsearch. Once the data is pushed into Elasticsearch, we use Kibana to analyze it. Using data analysis, we can track down any issue in the system. It helps us monitor and respond proactively in case of any issue. Here, we can fetch log data, application data, network data, and different system metrics data using Beats and Logstash, and we can apply data analysis. Many companies are using Elastic Stack for centralized data analysis to keep track of their running applications.

Application performance monitoring

Elastic Stack APM is an open-source application monitoring tool that has APM Server and APN Agents. The APM server is configured to receive data from APM agents and pass them to Elasticsearch. APM agents are language-specific agents that can be configured with the Elastic APM supported languages. Once configured, they start sending application metrics to the APM Server. Once the data is pushed to Elasticsearch, we can monitor it using Kibana. APM is very helpful for developers and system administrators, as they can monitor the performance and availability of the application using Elastic APM. Using APM, they can easily determine if there exists an issue in the system. We can also get the code details, so it makes code issues searchable in APM through the search feature of Elasticsearch. So, it provides us with the opportunity to improve the code quality by monitoring it. Elastic APM provides a custom UI on Kibana, using which we can monitor the application performance and create a custom dashboard in Kibana using APM data.

System performance monitoring

The system is a vital part of any running application, as the overall performance of the application is dependent on the system's performance. So, monitoring the system is necessary to avoid any surprises that can hamper performance. Many factors can affect application performance, such as CPU usage, memory usage, database performance, and so on. If we keep on monitoring these metrics, we can easily tackle a situation before it can adversely affect the application. We can configure Elastic Beats to get system metrics from different servers to Elasticsearch. Metricbeat can send system metrics data like CPU usage, memory usage, and so on. Packetbeats sends network packet details, and we can receive the uptime of services and APIs using heartbeat. We can configure these beats to receive the data, and once the data is in Elasticsearch, we can analyze it using Kibana. System Performance Monitoring is a common use case of Elasticsearch, as we always need to monitor the infrastructure on which the application is running.

Data Visualization

One more important use case of Elasticsearch is data visualization, as we collect data from different sources, save it to Elasticsearch, and then use different visualization tools to create the dashboards. Kibana, Grafana, or Graylog can be configured to visualize the Elasticsearch data. The data can be of any type and size; we just need to identify the key performance indicators, and we can plot them using any of the visualization tools.

Different clients for Elasticsearch

Elasticsearch provides us with REST APIs, using which we can communicate with Elasticsearch. However, it requires us to create a REST client, create the JSON query, and execute the query using the REST client. Apart from writing the Elasticsearch queries, we can use the following Elasticsearch clients, which are from different programming languages:

- Java
- PHP
- Perl
- Python
- .NET
- Ruby
- JavaScript
- Go

Using these language-specific Elasticsearch clients, we can interact with Elasticsearch in that language itself. It provides us with a way where we need not learn anything different to interact with Elasticsearch. Now, let's look at how to interact with Elasticsearch using these clients. We won't go into the details of these clients, but let's get a brief introduction.

Java

Java clients are of two types:

- Low-level REST client
- High-level REST client

Low-level clients can be used to interact through HTTP with the Elasticsearch cluster. On the other hand, a high-level REST client is built using a low-level client, and it exposes the APIs. These clients send the request by converting data into a byte-stream, and this process is known as marshalling. The response is shown to the user by converting the byte-stream to data, which is known as unmarshalling.

PHP

Elasticsearch PHP client is a low-level client that works like any other REST API. In PHP client, we created the associative arrays for different operations like indexing, searching, and so on. For example, if we want to index a document after creating the client, we must execute the following code snippet:

```
$index_data = [
```

```
  'index' => 'index_name',
   'id' => 'id',
   'body' => ['field_name' => 'field_value']
];
$response = $client->index($index_data);
```

Don't worry if you're unable to understand the code; it is for users who know PHP programming.

Perl

For Perl, Elasticsearch has a `Search::Elasticsearch` client, using which we can interact with Elasticsearch from a Perl program. After creating the Elasticsearch client, we can index a document using the following code snippet:

```
$client->index(
    index   => 'index_name',
    id      => 'id',
    body    => {
        'field_name' => 'field_value'
    }
);
```

Python

The Elasticsearch Python client translates Python data type to and from JSON, as Elasticsearch accepts JSON data. Python developers can code in Python and interact with Elasticsearch. If we want to index a document using Python client after creating it, we must write the following code snippet:

```
es.index(index = "my-index", id = "id", body = {
    'field_name' : 'field_value'
})
```

.NET

We have two .NET clients for Elasticsearch: Elasticsearch.Net and NEST. Elasticsearch.Net is a low-level client, while NEST is a high-level client. After creating the client, if we want to index a document using the .Net client, the following code snippet must be written.

Let's say we are creating a POCO object employee:

```
var Employee = new Employee
{
    Id = 1,
    FirstName = "Anurag",
    LastName = "Srivastava"
};

var indexResponse = client.IndexDocument(employee);
```

Ruby

For Ruby, Elasticsearch has a Rubygem client, using which we can interact with Elasticsearch. After creating the Elasticsearch client, we can index a document using the following code snippet:

```
client.index index: 'index_name', id: 'id', body: { field_name: 'field_value' }
```

JavaScript

Elasticsearch provides an official Node.js client for JavaScript. We can index a document by executing the following code snippet after creating the Elasticsearch client:

```
await client.index({
   index: 'index_name',
   body: {
      field_name: 'field_value'
    }
})
```

This way, we can configure the client and interact with Elasticsearch to index the documents, search them, and so on. We have covered some of the clients here. There are more clients, but discussing every client is out of the scope of this book.

How to use Elasticsearch

Till now, we discussed how Elasticsearch can be used to search data after indexing, but it is a search engine primarily used for data search. So, the question here is, "Can we use Elasticsearch instead of the database, and if not, how and why we should implement Elasticsearch along with a database?." To answer this question, we should understand the requirements and ask some questions, like "Are we going to use transactions or anything that is not well supported in Elasticsearch? For example, if we have a blog site where users can add blogs, and we need to search them to fetch the relevant blog, Elasticsearch can serve the purpose easily without any other database. Based on the types of requirements, we can categorize the use of Elasticsearch in the following groups:

- Elasticsearch as a primary data source
- Elasticsearch as a secondary data source for searching
- Elasticsearch as a standalone system

Now, let's discuss them in detail to understand how Elasticsearch fits into different types of requirement.

Elasticsearch as a primary data source

Elasticsearch has some issues on heavy load, and we can use it if we understand the risks associated while using it as a primary data source. We can use Elasticsearch as a primary data source if minor data loss is not a problem for the application. But again, that is a case where we have a heavy load. For search-intensive applications where less data update is required, we can use Elasticsearch without any other data storage tool. For example, if we have a blog website where the rate of blog creation or update is lower than the rate of blog searchs and views, Elasticsearch is suitable as a primary data source. It reduces the application's complexity, as Elasticsearch can show the search results quickly, and we need not add any database. Data indexing and search can be performed directly from Elasticsearch. The following image illustrates this:

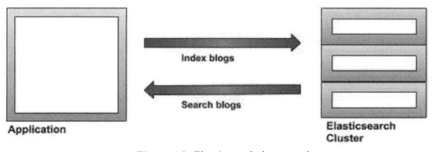

Figure 1.2: Elasticsearch data search

The preceding image shows the blog application using Elasticsearch as a primary data storage, where new blogs are getting indexed and searched from the Elasticsearch cluster. This way, we are fulfilling the database requirement using Elasticsearch, and the additional effort to pull data from a database and push it to Elasticsearch is removed. We can overcome data loss using multiple nodes and redundancy. Also, a blog website primarily needs a strong search engine, using which we can apply relevant search and analytics, and so on. Elasticsearch is well suited for this purpose. So, the idea is to identify the use cases where we can use Elasticsearch as a primary data source.

Elasticsearch as a secondary data source for searching

This is the most common and ideal use of Elasticsearch, as the primary database provides data storage while Elasticsearch is used for data search. We index data into Elasticsearch in parallel to other databases, or it is configured separately where Elasticsearch is synced with the primary database. The primary RDBMS database provides all the required features, such as transactions and relationships.

All new data or updates directly go to the primary database, and then they go to the secondary database, that is, Elasticsearch. This process can be done sequentially where we will push data into the primary as well as secondary data source or through any other data synchronization mechanism like the Elasticsearch plugin, Logstash, or any other third-party tool. I have also used this approach in many running applications. The idea is to improve the performance of a running system, as an already running system may need improvement, and we can use Elasticsearch there. Suppose an application is running with an RDBMS system where data is inserted into the database and can also be fetched from there. RDBMS is good for handling data and smooth transactions, but it's not as suitable for data search. So, we must implement Elasticsearch if we want to apply a full-text search on the application.

Now, the first challenge is to configure the Elasticsearch cluster and push all the data there so that we can apply the search using Elasticsearch. This can be done using any synchronization tool, such as the Elasticsearch plugin or Logstash. We can also configure the code to sequentially write data on both data sources. This architectural decision can be taken based on the requirements, but let's assume that we have configured a system to sync the data from primary RDBMS to secondary Elasticsearch. In this case, there would be a slight delay in the search, as it would take some time to index the document in Elasticsearch after it is inserted into the RDBMS system. The following image will help you understand the architecture of a system where we can use Elasticsearch as a secondary data source:

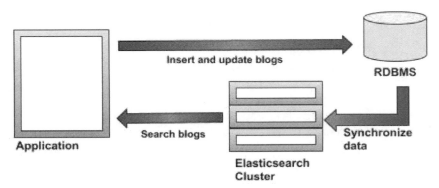

Figure 1.3: Elasticsearch RDBMS synchronization and data search

Here, we can see that new blog data is inserted into the database, and the data is updated into the database if there's any change in the blog. The data is synchronized with Elasticsearch after it is inserted or updated into the database. Once the data is synchronized, Elasticsearch can be used to perform the search.

Elasticsearch as a standalone system

We use Elasticsearch as a secondary database, primarily for search operation. That said, we can build a system for log analysis, dashboarding, monitoring, and security analysis, and so on using Elasticsearch. Elasticsearch, along with other tools of Elastic Stack, provides us with a great tool for performing data analysis on structured data as well as unstructured data. This data can be from any source such as system log, network packet data, system metrics, or database. The following image will help you understand how Elastic Stack can work together for data analysis:

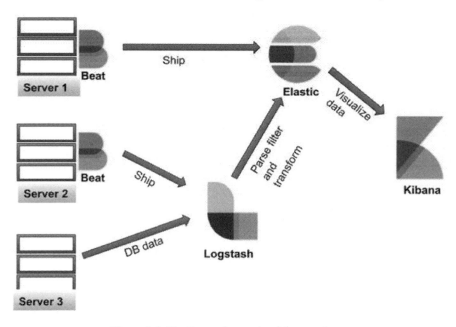

Figure 1.4: Elasticsearch as a standalone system

We can see that Beats can be configured on any server, from where they can send data to Logstash or directly to Elasticsearch. We'll cover Beats, Logstash, and Kibana, in chapter 3 "Working with Elastic Stack". Logstash can also be configured to read data from any database server like RDBMS or NoSQL. Beats and Logstash push the data to Elasticsearch, which works as a storage tool in Elastic Stack and is also known as the heart of Elastic Stack. Once the data is stored in Elasticsearch, we can use Kibana for data analysis and visualization. This way, Elasticsearch can be configured to work as a standalone system to solve various problems.

Conclusion

This chapter provided an introduction to Elasticsearch, and we discussed why search is important, along with the different use case of data search. We also discussed the basic concepts of Elasticsearch like node, cluster, documents, index, and shards. Then, we went through different Elasticsearch use cases such as data search, data logging and analysis, application performance monitoring, system performance monitoring, and data visualization. We also looked at Elasticsearch clients, and then we moved on to understand how to use Elasticsearch as a primary data source, a secondary data source, and as a standalone system.

The next chapter will walk you through the installation of Elasticsearch on different platforms and the REST APIs that it provides.

Questions

1. What is Elasticsearch, and where we can use it?

2. How many types of nodes are there in Elasticsearch?

3. What are Elasticsearch clients, and what are the different languages they support?

4. Use an Elasticsearch language client, and try to use it in your programming language.

5. Explain different use cases of Elasticsearch.

CHAPTER 2
Installing Elasticsearch

Introduction

In the last chapter, we looked at why data search is important and covered various use cases of data search. Then, we covered the basics of Elasticsearch, like the different components, use cases, and different clients supported in Elasticsearch. We also discussed how we can use Elasticsearch as a primary data source, as a secondary data source, and as a standalone system. Now, let's move on to understanding what is new in Elasticsearch 7.x, after which we will cover the installation of Elasticsearch 7.5 on different platforms. After installation, we will explore the REST APIs of Elasticsearch.

Structure

In this chapter, we will discuss the following topics:

- What's new in Elasticsearch 7.x?
- Installing Elasticsearch
- Starting the Elasticsearch service and verifying
- Elasticsearch REST APIs

Objectives

After studying this unit, you should be able to:

- Understand the features of Elasticsearch 7.x
- Install Elasticsearch
- Perform REST queries on Elasticsearch

What's new in Elasticsearch 7.x

There are various improvements in Elasticsearch version 7.x, which have enhanced performance. We cannot discuss all of them, but let's look at some important improvements in Elasticsearch version 7.x.

Adaptive replica selection

In adaptive replica selection, the nodes keep track of other nodes and compare their performance for long search requests. Using this information, the nodes decide on the frequency of request to send on other nodes. This feature was added for experimentation in version 6.1, and the option was disabled in version 6.x. In version 7.x, the feature is enabled by default . So, search requests are now forwarded to the nodes that can handle them better instead of round-robin fashion.

Skip shard refreshes

Before Elasticsearch version 7.x, the indices were refreshed automatically by default every second, in the background. This ensured that Elasticsearch search results could be available within one second after indexing. This feature is good, but it impacts the indexing performance, and it is unnecessary if no search operation is performed. This issue has been resolved in Elasticsearch 7.0 onward by identifying if a shard is "search idle". A shard can be search idle if there is no search request on it for 30 seconds. If a shard is a search idle, Elasticsearch will stop the scheduled refresh. If a search request occurs, the refresh will start and continue until it is idle for 30 seconds again. There is only one catch; it will happen only if we have not changed the default refresh interval set. This behavior of Elasticsearch has improved indexing performance.

One shard per index by default

Before Elasticsearch 7.x, there were, by default, five shards per index, but it has now been changed to one shard per index by default. As this was default, people often forget to change it, which could impact performance. Based on the number of indices, the shard count becomes five times, which is not recommended at times. Here, the default one shard per index is a very good move because it will reduce the overhead, and if anyone wants more shards for the index, the same can be configured for that index.

Support for small heap

A new circuit breaker feature has been added in Elasticsearch 7.0 onward; it ensures that requests are rejected if reserved plus actual heap size exceeds 95%. So, Elasticsearch circuit breaker checks the total memory usage of JVM and saves us from the out-of-memory issue. It ensures that the cluster remains active even when we have excess loads. These are some main improved features of Elasticsearch 7.x. Now, let's understand how to install Elasticsearch on different platforms.

Installing Elasticsearch

Before jumping to the Elasticsearch API and other details, we should know how to install Elasticsearch on different platforms. Here, we will cover the installation process of Elasticsearch on different platforms.

Installing Elasticsearch on Linux or macOS

Elasticsearch provides a .tar.gz archive for the Linux and macOS, which is free under the Elastic license. It contains both the open-source as well as commercial features. If we want to use the commercial features, we must purchase the license. We can also opt for a 30-days trial of the commercial features. We can find the latest stable version of Elasticsearch on the Download Elasticsearch page on the Elastic website. Let's take the example of Elasticsearch 7.5.2.

Installing Elasticsearch on Linux

To install Elasticsearch on Linux, we must do the following:

- First, we need to download the Elasticsearch 7.5.0 Linux tar file. Then, we must run the following command:

  ```
  wget https://artifacts.elastic.co/downloads/elasticsearch/
  elasticsearch-7.5.2-linux-x86_64.tar.gz
  ```

- After downloading the archive, we can compare the SHA using the published checksum. For the comparison, we need to execute the following commands:

  ```
  wget https://artifacts.elastic.co/downloads/elasticsearch/
  elasticsearch-7.5.2-linux-x86_64.tar.gz.sha512
  shasum -a 512 -c elasticsearch-7.5.2-linux-x86_64.tar.gz.sha512
  ```

- After downloading and comparing the checksum, we have to extract the archive using the following command:

```
tar -xzf elasticsearch-7.5.2-linux-x86_64.tar.gz
cd elasticsearch-7.5.2/
```

- After extracting the archive, we can see the extracted directory structure inside the Elasticsearch home directory. Now, we must start the Elasticsearch service by running the following command:

```
./bin/elasticsearch
```

Installing Elasticsearch on macOS

To install Elasticsearch on macOS, we need to do the following:

- First, we must download the Elasticsearch 7.5.0 macOS tar file using the following command:

```
wget https://artifacts.elastic.co/downloads/elasticsearch/
elasticsearch-7.5.2-darwin-x86_64.tar.gz
```

- After downloading the archive, we can compare the SHA using the published checksum. For the comparison, we need to execute the following commands:

```
wget https://artifacts.elastic.co/downloads/elasticsearch/
elasticsearch-7.5.2-darwin-x86_64.tar.gz.sha512
shasum -a 512 -c elasticsearch-7.5.2-darwin-x86_64.tar.gz.sha512
```

- After downloading and comparing the checksum, we have to extract the archive using the following command:

```
tar -xzf elasticsearch-7.5.2-darwin-x86_64.tar.gz
cd elasticsearch-7.5.2/
```

- After extracting the archive, we can see the extracted directory structure inside the Elasticsearch home directory. Now, we must start the Elasticsearch service by running the following command:

```
./bin/elasticsearch
```

We can start the Elasticsearch service using the preceding command. Now, we will look at how to install Elasticsearch using the Debian package.

Installing Elasticsearch using the Debian package

On Debian-based systems like Debian and Ubuntu, we can install Elasticsearch using the Debian package of Elasticsearch. We can download the Debian package from the download section of the Elastic website. This package is free, and we can test the commercial features for 30 days after installing Elasticsearch if we opt for the trial. We must follow these steps to install Elasticsearch using Debian package:

- We must install the public signing key after downloading it using the following expression:

```
wget -qO - https://artifacts.elastic.co/GPG-KEY-elasticsearch |
sudo apt-key add -
```

- After installing the public signing key, we need to install the apt-transport-https package using the following command:

```
sudo apt-get install apt-transport-https
```

- Then, we need to save the repository definition at the /etc/apt/sources.list.d/elastic-7.x.list file. We must run the following command for saving the repository definition:

```
echo "deb https://artifacts.elastic.co/packages/7.x/apt stable
main" | sudo tee -a /etc/apt/sources.list.d/elastic-7.x.list
```

- Now, we can install the Elasticsearch Debian package using the following command:

```
sudo apt-get update && sudo apt-get install elasticsearch
```

Installing the Debian package manually

We can also manually download and install the Debian package of Elasticsearch by following these steps:

- First, we need to download the Elasticsearch 7.5.2 Debian package file using the following command:

```
wget https://artifacts.elastic.co/downloads/elasticsearch/
elasticsearch-7.5.2-amd64.deb
```

- After downloading the Debian package, we can compare the SHA using the published checksum. For the comparison, we must execute the following commands:

```
wget https://artifacts.elastic.co/downloads/elasticsearch/
elasticsearch-7.5.2-amd64.deb.sha512

shasum -a 512 -c elasticsearch-7.5.2-amd64.deb.sha512
```

- After downloading and comparing the checksum, we have to extract the archive using the following command:

```
sudo dpkg -i elasticsearch-7.5.2-amd64.deb
```

The preceding command shows how we can install the Debian package of Elasticsearch manually.

Installing Elasticsearch using the RPM package

On RPM-based systems like OpenSuSE, SLES, Centos, Red Hat, and Oracle Enterprise, we can install Elasticsearch using the RPM package of Elasticsearch. We can download the RPM package from the download section of the Elastic website. The RPM package is also free, and we can test the commercial features for 30 days after installing Elasticsearch. Follow these steps to install Elasticsearch using the RPM package:

- First, we need to install the Elasticsearch public signing key after downloading it. The following command installs the public signing key:

```
rpm --import https://artifacts.elastic.co/GPG-KEY-elasticsearch
```

- We need to create the elasticsearch.repo file under the /etc/yum.repos.d/ directory for the RedHat-based distributions. In this file, we must add the following:

```
[elasticsearch]
name=Elasticsearch repository for 7.x packages
baseurl=https://artifacts.elastic.co/packages/7.x/yum
gpgcheck=1
gpgkey=https://artifacts.elastic.co/GPG-KEY-elasticsearch
enabled=0
autorefresh=1
type=rpm-md
```

- We must save the file after adding the preceding content. Then, we're all set to install Elasticsearch using RPM. We must execute the following command to install Elasticsearch on different environments, as the command can vary on different platforms:

    o For CentOS and older Red Hat-based distributions, we need to run the following command:

    ```
    sudo yum install elasticsearch
    ```

    o For Fedora and other newer Red Hat distributions, we must run the following command:

    ```
    sudo dnf install elasticsearch
    ```

    o For OpenSUSE-based distributions, the following command must be run:

    ```
    sudo zypper install elasticsearch
    ```

This way, we can install Elasticsearch using the RPM package.

Installing the RPM package manually

We can also install Elasticsearch manually using the RPM package, and the same can be done in the following steps:

- First, we must download the Elasticsearch 7.6.0 RPM file using the following command:

```
wget https://artifacts.elastic.co/downloads/elasticsearch/
elasticsearch-7.6.0-x86_64.rpm
```

- After downloading the RPM, we can compare the SHA using the published checksum. For the comparison, we need to execute the following commands:

```
wget https://artifacts.elastic.co/downloads/elasticsearch/
elasticsearch-7.6.0-x86_64.rpm.sha512

shasum -a 512 -c elasticsearch-7.6.0-x86_64.rpm.sha512
```

- After downloading and comparing the checksum, we have to extract the archive using the following command:

```
sudo rpm --install elasticsearch-7.6.0-x86_64.rpm
```

This way, we can manually install Elasticsearch using RPM.

Start the Elasticsearch service and verify

We can test whether Elasticsearch node is running by sending the HTTP GET request on Elasticsearch host and port. For example, if we have installed Elasticsearch on a local machine, we can test this by hitting the following URL:

```
curl -X GET "localhost:9200/"
```

The preceding URL will get the following response if Elasticsearch is running:

```
{
  "name" : "KELLGGNLPTP0305",
  "cluster_name" : "elasticsearch",
  "cluster_uuid" : "BIP_9t5fR-SxB72hLM8SwA",
  "version" : {
    "number" : "7.6.0",
    "build_flavor" : "default",
    "build_type" : "deb",
    "build_hash" : "7f634e9f44834fbc12724506cc1da681b0c3b1e3",
    "build_date" : "2020-02-06T00:09:00.449973Z",
    "build_snapshot" : false,
```

```
    "lucene_version" : "8.4.0",
    "minimum_wire_compatibility_version" : "6.8.0",
    "minimum_index_compatibility_version" : "6.0.0-beta1"
  },
  "tagline": "You Know, for Search."
}
```

Elasticsearch REST APIs

Elasticsearch supports REST-based APIs, in which we use JSON to communicate over HTTP. Using REST APIs, we can perform different operations like viewing the status of index, cluster, shard, and so on, changing the settings, creating and deleting an index, or adding or deleting documents. Basically, we can perform all operations using REST APIs. Generally, all REST APIs support multi-index, which means if we apply the comma-separated index names in parameter, it will operate on those indices. We can apply _all in the parameter in case we want the query to be performed on all indices. We can also exclude specific indices by adding a minus sign before the index name. Index parameter also supports wildcard names, where we can match multiple indices. We can append pretty=true in any REST API to return a formatted JSON. Also, we can get the results in a YAML format by appending the `format=yaml` option. Now, let's look at the different operations we can perform using REST APIs.

cat APIs

Elasticsearch provides us with the APIs to get all details, but they provide JSON data, which is often not very good to see the status. For example, if we want to see the cluster health status, it is better to get the snapshot instead of a JSON document to explore. Elasticsearch cat API helps us achieve that, and we can get the numbers that are important to us. We can get the health status of cluster, indices, shard, and so on using cat API, and it also lists all the indices. Let's discuss the different options of cat APIs.

cat API parameters

There are some common parameters we can use with the cat API, like verbose, using which we can add headers in the output. We can get the details of fields for the command using the help option, we can provide the field name to get in the output using headers, we can change the format of the output using the response format option, and we can sort the data using the sort option. We will cover each of these in detail as they are very handy and useful.

Verbose

By default, the results of any command are shown without any header, which makes it difficult to understand. Using the verbose option, we can show the headers of the results. For example, if we run the following command:

```
curl -XGET "http://localhost:9200/_cat/nodes"
```

It will return the following output:

```
127.0.0.1 62 97 97 4.44 4.46 4.47 dilm * ANURAGLPTP0305
```

In the preceding output, it is not easy to identify all the fields, so we can add the verbose option in the parameter, For this, we need to add ?v with API endpoint, so the query will look as follows:

```
curl -XGET "http://localhost:9200/_cat/nodes?v"
```

After executing the preceding URL, we will get the following output:

```
ip           heap.percent ram.percent cpu load_1m load_5m load_15m node.
role master name
127.0.0.1              51          97 98    4.60    4.51     4.49 dilm
*        ANURAGLPTP0305
```

In the initial query response, we can see details like the IP address, heap percentage, RAM percentage, CPU load, node role, and master name, and so on. The header will not be visible if we don't use ?v.

Help

If we pass the **help** option as a parameter in any command, it will output the details of the fields. For example, if we run the following command:

```
curl -XGET "http://localhost:9200/_cat/master?v"
```

It will return the following output:

```
id                      host      ip        node
OsuaWgbGQd2KXbWE3ENfEg 127.0.0.1 127.0.0.1 ANURAGLPTP0305
```

Now, we have to append the help option as a parameter if we want to see the field details. So, we have to write the API URL as follows:

```
curl -XGET "http://localhost:9200/_cat/master?v&help"
```

After executing the preceding URL, we will get the following output:

```
id      |    | node id
host    | h  | host name
```

```
ip       |   |   ip address
node     | n |   node name
```

In the initial help response, we can see the description for the header fields. It helps us understand the response the command is returning.

Headers

We can pass the header fields in each of the cat commands to show only those fields in the output. For example, we can write the following expression if we want to pick only the IP address and CPU from nodes command:

```
curl -XGET "http://localhost:9200/_cat/nodes?v&h=ip,cpu"
```

After executing the preceding URL, we will get the following output:

```
ip              cpu
127.0.0.1       61
```

In the preceding response, we can see the desired ip and CPU header columns, and for that, the same is mentioned in the query. So, whenever we want to see only certain fields, we can pass them using the h parameter.

Response formats

We can change the output format of the API by providing the format option of the parameter. We can set JSON, text, YAML, smile, or cbor format based on the requirement. For example, we can list the indices in the text format using the following command:

```
curl -XGET "http://localhost:9200/_cat/indices?v"
```

The preceding command will provide the following output:

```
health status index                          uuid
pri rep docs.count docs.deleted store.size pri.store.size
yellow open twitter                        n8JfARF-R_63_5noIn9TzA 1
1       2     0    4.8kb    4.8kb
```

Now, we must change the format to JSON if we want to output the same result in JSON. Refer to the following expression:

```
curl -XGET "http://localhost:9200/_cat/indices?format=json"
```

After executing the preceding command, we will get the following output:

```
{
    "health" : "yellow",
    "status" : "open",
```

```
    "index" : "twitter",
    "uuid" : "n8JfARF-R_63_5noIn9TzA",
    "pri" : "1",
    "rep" : "1",
    "docs.count" : "2",
    "docs.deleted" : "0",
    "store.size" : "4.8kb",
    "pri.store.size" : "4.8kb"
}
```

The same result can also be converted to YAML by changing the format option of the parameter to YAML. It will provide the following output:

```
- health: "yellow"
  status: "open"
  index: "twitter"
  uuid: "n8JfARF-R_63_5noIn9TzA"
  pri: "1"
  rep: "1"
  docs.count: "2"
  docs.deleted: "0"
  store.size: "4.8kb"
  pri.store.size: "4.8kb"
```

It also supports the smile and cbor formats, which are binary serialization of the generic JSON data model.

Sort

Each command also supports sorting, where we have to provide the field name to sort and the order in which we want the sorting. For sorting, we must add the s keyword with the equal sign, the field name with the colon sign, and the sorting order. Refer to the following expression:

```
curl -XGET "http://localhost:9200/_cat/templates?v&s=version:desc,order"
```

After executing the preceding command, we will get the following output:

```
name                    index_patterns              order   version
packetbeat-6.5.2        [packetbeat-6.5.2-*]        1
packetbeat-6.2.2        [packetbeat-6.2.2-*]        1
metricbeat-7.3.0        [metricbeat-7.3.0-*]        1
```

We can see the listing in the preceding response, and this listing is sorted using the s keyword.

cat count API

Using the cat count API, we can count the number of documents in a single index or all indices. The format of cat count API is as follows:

```
GET /_cat/count/<index>
```

```
GET /_cat/count
```

The first expression counts the document of a single index, while the second expression counts the documents for all the indices. For example, refer to the following expression:

```
GET /_cat/count?v
```

Using the preceding expression, we can get the following output:

```
epoch        timestamp count
1582645351 15:42:31   11824319
```

This way, we can get the total document count for all the available indices.

cat health API

We can get the health status of a cluster using the cat health API. It is similar to the cluster health API, and the format of the cat health API is as follows:

```
GET /_cat/health
```

If we want to get the cluster health using cat health API, we must run the following command:

```
curl -X GET "localhost:9200/_cat/health?v&pretty"
```

The output of the preceding expression is as follows:

```
epoch        timestamp cluster        status node.total node.data shards
pri relo init unassign pending_tasks max_task_wait_time active_shards_
percent
1582646292 15:58:12   elasticsearch yellow          1         1
200 200   0   0       87                 0                  -
69.7%
```

Here, we can see the health details of the cluster, such as total nodes, data nodes, shard details, pending tasks, and so on.

cat indices API

Using the cat indices API, we can get high-level information for the indices of a cluster. If we want to list all the indices of a cluster, we must run the following command:

```
curl -XGET "http://localhost:9200/_cat/indices?v"
```

We will get the following response:

```
health status index                                     uuid
pri rep docs.count docs.deleted store.size pri.store.size
yellow open    players                            ljylFwacRniKzW2j1N-dPA
1   1          6              0       27.6kb      27.6kb
yellow open    mappingtest3                       aQaGqoBARL-7dFYFgfak8A
1   1          2              0       8.4kb       8.4kb
yellow open    my_index_stan                      EYUj59KTSs6GznogUl9dxA
1   1          0              0       283b         283b
```

Here, we can see the indices details of the cluster, such as `health`, `status`, `index name`, `uuid`, `primary count`, `replica count`, `document count`, `deleted document count`, `store size`, and so on.

cat master API

Using this API, we can get the details of the master node. We must execute the following command to get the master node information:

```
curl -XGET "http://localhost:9200/_cat/master?v"
```

We will get the following response:

```
OsuaWgbGQd2KXbWE3ENfEg 127.0.0.1 127.0.0.1 ANURAGLPTP0305
```

In the preceding response, we can see the master node details of the cluster, such as node id, IP address, cluster name, and so on.

cat nodes API

Using this API, we can get the details of the cluster's nodes. We need to execute the following command to get the cluster's nodes information:

```
curl -XGET "http://localhost:9200/_cat/nodes?v"
```

We will get the following response:

```
ip          heap.percent ram.percent cpu load_1m load_5m load_15m node.
role master name
127.0.0.1            52           90 77    4.62    4.49     4.59 dilm
*       ANURAGLPTP0305
```

In the preceding response, we can see the node details of the cluster, such as IP address, heap percentage, RAM percentage, CPU load, and so on.

cat shards API

The shard API of cat provides us with the details about different nodes and their shards, like whether they are primary or replica, total bytes they took on disk, and the number of documents. To get the shard details, we must execute the following command:

```
curl -XGET "http://localhost:9200/_cat/shards?v"
```

We will get the following response:

```
index                            shard prirep state        docs
store ip              node
chocolates                       0     p      STARTED      4
14.6kb 127.0.0.1      ANURAGLPTP0305
chocolates                       0     r      UNASSIGNED
```

Till now, we covered cat APIs, which are good for status which are, generally numerical values in text format. We can easily get the required information using this. Now, let's explore some cluster APIs.

Cluster APIs

Cluster-level APIs are applied on nodes of the cluster, and they provide details of nodes stats, info, and so on. Now, let's discuss some cluster APIs.

Cluster health API

We can get the health status of the cluster using the cluster health API. This API returns the result in JSON format, unlike the cat API. We must execute the following command to get the cluster health status:

```
curl -XGET "http://localhost:9200/_cluster/health"
```

We will get the following response:

```
{
  "cluster_name" : "elasticsearch",
  "status" : "yellow",
  "timed_out" : false,
  "number_of_nodes" : 1,
  "number_of_data_nodes" : 1,
```

```
  "active_primary_shards" : 202,
  "active_shards" : 202,
  "relocating_shards" : 0,
  "initializing_shards" : 0,
  "unassigned_shards" : 87,
  "delayed_unassigned_shards" : 0,
  "number_of_pending_tasks" : 0,
  "number_of_in_flight_fetch" : 0,
  "task_max_waiting_in_queue_millis" : 0,
  "active_shards_percent_as_number" : 69.8961937716263
}
```

This way, we can get a JSON document for cluster health.

Cluster stats API

This API returns the statistics of the cluster, using which we can get different details like index metrics and nodes metrics. In a single API, we get details such as shard numbers, memory usage, store size, JVM versions, CPU usage, OS, and so on. To get the cluster stats, we must run the following command:

```
curl -XGET "http://localhost:9200/_cluster/state/_all/twitter"
```

It will provide us the following JSON document:

```
{
  "cluster_name" : "elasticsearch",
  "cluster_uuid" : "BIP_9t5fR-SxB72hLM8SwA",
  "version" : 37326,
  "state_uuid" : "6L8zreS5T7GFWPIHWu972Q",
  "master_node" : "OsuaWgbGQd2KXbWE3ENfEg",
  "blocks" : {
    "indices" : {
      "index" : {
        "5" : {
          "description" : "index read-only (api)",
          "retryable" : false,
          "levels" : [
            "write",
```

```
                "metadata_write"
            ]
        }
    }
  }
},
"nodes" : {
  "OsuaWgbGQd2KXbWE3ENfEg" : {

    …….
  }
},
"metadata" : {
 "templates" : { },
  "indices" : {
    "twitter" : {
      "state" : "open",
      "settings" : {
        "index" : {

          …….. 
        }
      },
      "mappings" : {
        "_doc" : {
          "properties" : {

            …….. .
          }
        }
      },
      "aliases" : [ ],
      "primary_terms" : {
        "0" : 125
      },
      "in_sync_allocations" : {
        "0" : [
```

```
            "F0PQ_WKwQbaFqDFlC9ix8w"
          ]
        }
      }
    },
    "index-graveyard" : {
      "tombstones" : [ ]
    }
  },
  "routing_table" : {
    "indices" : {
      "twitter" : {
        "shards" : {
          "0" : [
              …….
          ]
        }
      }
    }
  },
  "routing_nodes" : {
    "unassigned" : [
      {
        …….
        "unassigned_info" : {
         ……..
        }
      }
    ],
    "nodes" : {
      "OsuaWgbGQd2KXbWE3ENfEg" : [
        {
          ……..
        }
```

```
        ]
      }
    }
}
```

The preceding result provides details such as cluster name, UUID, version, node details, metadata, and so on.

These were some of the basic APIs that we can use to get the required information. There are many other APIs for the index, documents, search, snapshot, and so on. We will go through them in the respective chapters of the book, so keep reading.

Conclusion

In this chapter, we started with what is new in Elasticsearch 7.x, and then we covered the installation of Elasticsearch on different platforms. We looked at Linux and macOS installation, and we then moved on to installing Elasticsearch using the Debian package and the RPM package. Then, we discussed how to install Elasticsearch using the MSI Windows installer. Then, we explored how to verify whether Elasticsearch is running on the system. After the installation process, we covered Elasticsearch REST APIs.

The next chapter will take you through Elastic Stack and its different components, such as Elasticsearch, Logstash, Kibana, and Beats. After the introduction, we will look at how these components work together.

Questions

1. What is new in Elasticsearch 7.x?

2. How to install Elasticsearch on different platforms

3. How to list all indices of Elasticsearch cluster

4. How to get the count of all documents in Elasticsearch

5. How to fetch the health status of the cluster

6. How to get the node details of Elasticsearch cluster

7. How to fetch the stats for the Elasticsearch cluster

CHAPTER 3
Working with Elastic Stack

Introduction

The last chapter introduced us to what's new in Elasticsearch 7.x, and then we installed Elasticsearch on different platforms. After installation, we covered Elasticsearch REST APIs. Now, we will cover Elastic Stack and its different components like Elasticsearch, Logstash, Kibana, and Beats. We will start with an introduction to different components of Elastic Stack, and then we will cover each of these components in detail. After the introduction, we will cover how these components work together for different use cases. So, let's start with an introduction to the different components of Elastic Stack.

Structure

In this chapter, we will cover the following:

- What is Elastic Stack?
- Elasticsearch
- Logstash
- Kibana
- Beats
- How each component works together

Objectives

After studying this unit, you should be able to:

- Understand what is Elastic Stack
- Understand the different components of Elastic Stack
- Understand how the components of Elastic Stack work together

What is Elastic Stack

Elastic Stack was initially known as ELK stack because of three open-source applications: Elasticsearch, Logstash, and Kibana. They are quite different in the use case, but they work exceptionally well together and solve various business problems when combined. The name was changed to Elastic Stack as many new tools like various Beats, APM, machine learning, and so on, were introduced.

Elastic Stack provides us with an end-to-end solution for data analysis that helps us in data search, analysis, and visualization. We can fetch different types of data like structured data, unstructured data, time-based, Geo data, or any other type of data. We can use Beats or Logstash to ingest this data into Elasticsearch, which is centralized storage and is known as the heart of Elastic Stack. Once the data is stored in Elasticsearch, we can use it for search and analysis. Using Kibana, we can create a visualization on top of Elasticsearch data and apply machine learning and so on. In Kibana, we can do a lot more, like configuring APM for application performance monitoring or using SIEM for security analysis.

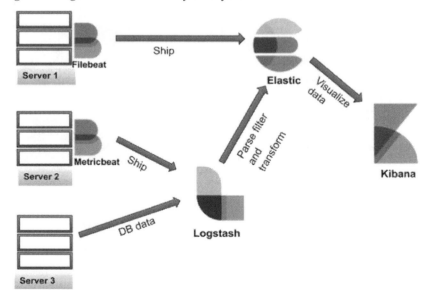

Figure 3.1: Elastic Stack

The preceding diagram depicts the use of Elastic Stack, where Beats are configured to fetch file data and metric data from servers. In contrast, Logstash is configured to fetch DB data and send it to Elasticsearch, while Filebeat is sending data directly to Elasticsearch. Beats can send data directly to Elasticsearch, or we can configure Logstash if we want data enrichment or modification before sending it to Elasticsearch. Now, let's discuss the different components of Elastic Stack.

Elasticsearch

We already covered Elasticsearch in the previous chapters, but to reiterate, Elasticsearch is an open-source, distributed, search and analytics engine. It can handle different types of data, such as textual data, numeric data, structured or unstructured data, geospatial data, and so on. It is built on top of Apache Lucene with the additional option of scalability and REST API for different operations. Elasticsearch is the central component of Elastic Stack, so it is also known as the heart of Elastic Stack. Elasticsearch was first released in 2010 by Elasticsearch N.V., which is now known as Elastic.

Logstash

Logstash is an open-source, data processing pipeline using which we can ingest data from different sources, transform it, and send it to different sources. We can also convert unstructured data into structured data, enrich data, transform it, and send it to multiple sources. We can use Logstash for the following purposes:

- To analyze structured and unstructured data and events.

- To connect with various types of input and output sources like a file, Beats, Kafka, DB, Elasticsearch, and so on.

- To transform data and store it for analysis.

- To fetch data from different sources, such as DB, CSV, and file.

Logstash is a data processing pipeline with three components: input, filter, and output. The input and output plugins are mandatory, while the filter plugin is optional, and we can use it when required. Input plugins are used to read data from different sources like DB, files, RDBMS, NoSQL, CSV, Kafka, and so on. On the other hand, filter plugins are used to modify the data before sending it to the output; here we can delete or add fields, update data types, convert unstructured data into structured data, perform basic calculations, and so on. And we can write data to different destinations like Elasticsearch, files, DB, and Kafka using output plugins.

The following diagram shows a Logstash pipeline:

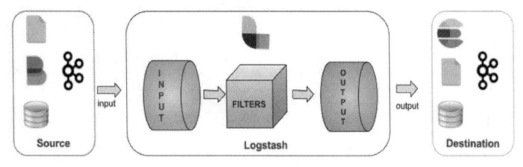

Figure 3.2: Logstash

We can see three blocks in the preceding diagram, where the first block shows the source from where Logstash is taking the input. The source block shows different tools and software like Kafka, Beats, File, Elasticsearch, S3, and DB, etc that can send data to Logstash. Then, we have the Logstash pipeline, where we can see the input, filter, and output plugins. Data is fetched through the input plugin, which reads it from various sources. The filter plugin then transforms the data and sends it to the output plugin, which sends it to different destinations. The third block shows the destination where Logstash output sends data. The destination block also shows different tools and software such as Kafka, Beats, File, DB, Elasticsearch, S3, HTTP, and NoSQL etc.

Logstash input plugin

Logstash provides various input plugins to read data from different sources. We can use them as per the requirement like if we want to read a file data, then we can use the file input plugin while if the data source is Beats, then we need to use the Beats plugin. We have many Logstash input plugins; some of them are as follows:

- Stdin
- Beats
- Cloudwatch
- Github
- RabbitMQ
- SQLite
- TCP
- Twitter
- File
- MongoDB

- Elasticsearch
- JDBC
- Redis
- Kafka
- Http

These were some of the input plugins of Logstash. Logstash supports many more plugins, but we have listed the important once here.

Logstash filter plugin

Using Logstash filter plugins, we can transform the original data and do multiple things like converting unstructured complex data into a simple structured format that can easily be searched. We can also add additional details like geo data using the IP address field or remove unnecessary fields from the data. Some of the Logstash filter plugins are as follows:

- GeoIP
- CSV
- JDBC
- Date
- Grok
- JSON
- XML
- Date
- DNS
- Elasticsearch
- HTTP
- Mutate
- Ruby
- Split
- UUID
- Translate

These were some of the Logstash filter plugins. Logstash supports many more plugins, but these are a few important ones.

Logstash output plugin

Logstash provides various output plugins to send data to various destinations, and we can use them as per our requirement. For example, if we want to send data to Elasticsearch, we should use the Elasticsearch output plugin, and a file output plugin is to be used if we want to send it to a file. Some of the Logstash output plugins are as follows:

- File
- Stdout
- MongoDB
- Elasticsearch
- Redis
- Kafka
- Http
- Nagios
- S3
- Cloudwatch
- CSV
- Datadog
- Email
- RabbitMQ
- Redmine
- SQS
- TCP
- UDP

There are many more plugins that help us with different use cases using Logstash. Now that we've discussed the input, filter, and output plugins of Logstash, let's see how we can use them to create a pipeline using which data can be imported, filtered, and sent to a destination using the output plugin. For that, we must create the Logstash configuration file, and the following is the format for the same:

```
input
{
    .........
}
filter
{
```

```
.........
}
output
{
    .........
}
```

In the preceding Logstash configuration format, we can see the input, filter, and output sections. Under the input section, we must mention the name of the input plugin to read the data from any input source. Under the filter section, we have to provide the name of the filter plugin to be used to transform the data. Under the output section, we have to mention the output filter name using which we can send the data to a destination. This way, we can create a Logstash configuration file and start ingesting data.

We can test the Logstash pipeline without creating the configuration file, by using the following command:

```
bin/logstash -e 'input { stdin { } } output { stdout {} }'
```

We can easily test the Logstash pipeline with this command, as we can provide the input plugin as standard input and the output plugin as standard output. After hitting the preceding command, we can write any text that Logstash will capture through stdin and output the same on the screen using the stdout output plugin. Take a look at the following screenshot for the execution of the preceding command:

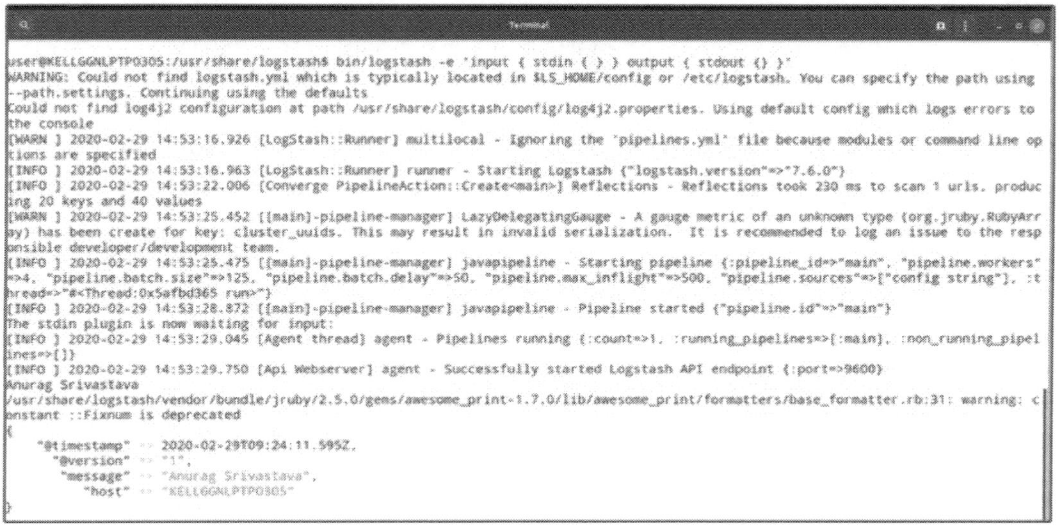

Figure 3.3: Execution response of Logstash pipeline

The preceding screenshot illustrates the Logstash pipeline using `stdin` as the input plugin and `stdout` as the output plugin. It will output the data we type using the keyboard on standard input.

This way, we can test the Logstash pipeline; but we must create a Logstash configuration file that we can save inside the `/logstash/conf.d/` directory to process different input and output. For example, if we want to do the same input and output pipeline using a configuration file, we can create a file and copy the code block of the input and output section over there. For example, let's say the file name is `standard_input_output.conf`. So, we need to write the following code in the Logstash configuration file:

```
input
{
 stdin { }
}
output
{
stdout {}
}
```

Now, we can execute the Logstash configuration file by executing the following command:

bin/logstash -f /etc/logstash/conf.d/crimes.conf

The preceding command is executed on the Ubuntu operating system, and the **conf.d** directory can vary based on the operating system. So, we can execute the Logstash pipeline using the preceding command. Refer to the following screenshot:

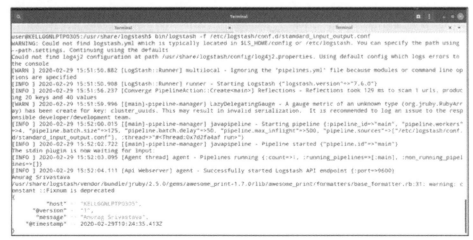

Figure 3.4: *Execution response of the Logstash configuration file.*

The preceding screenshot illustrates the Logstash pipeline using a Logstash configuration file. For different input and output processing, we can create different configuration files. On starting the Logstash service, the configuration files would be executed, and we can also execute the files manually using the preceding command.

Fetch Apache logs using logstash

We can fetch data from different sources using Logstash, such as MySQL, MongoDB, CSV, files, Elasticsearch, and so on. To fetch data from these sources, we have to use the respective input plugins of Logstash. We cannot cover everything in this book, but let's take a simple use case to understand how we can process data using Logstash. Apache access log is unstructured data, and we need to process it to make it searchable. Here's the Apache log entry:

```
127.0.0.1 - - [29/Feb/2020:18:43:46 +0530] "GET /test/admin.php
HTTP/1.1" 200 2159 "-" "Mozilla/5.0 (X11; Ubuntu; Linux x86_64; rv:72.0)
Gecko/20100101 Firefox/72.0"

127.0.0.1 - - [29/Feb/2020:18:43:47 +0530] "GET /test/admin.
php?file=default.css&version=4.2.5&driver=mysql HTTP/1.1" 200 2343
"http://localhost/test/admin.php" "Mozilla/5.0 (X11; Ubuntu; Linux
x86_64; rv:72.0) Gecko/20100101 Firefox/72.0"

127.0.0.1 - - [29/Feb/2020:18:43:47 +0530] "GET /test/adminer.css
HTTP/1.1" 200 4883 "http://localhost/test/admin.php" "Mozilla/5.0 (X11;
Ubuntu; Linux x86_64; rv:72.0) Gecko/20100101 Firefox/72.0"
```

Now, let's process the Apache logs using Logstash. We will use the Logstash file input plugin for this, and we will provide the path of the Apache log file. As these logs are unstructured, we need to format them in a structured format before writing them to Elasticsearch. For filtering, we can use the grok pattern to write our custom regular expression, or we can use the predefined patterns of Logstash. Here, we will use the COMBINEDAPACHELOG pattern to process the Apache logs. Let's create the apache_data.conf Apache log configuration file and write the following code:

```
input {
    file {
        path => "/var/log/apache2/access.log"
        type => "apache_access"
    }
}
filter {
  grok {
    match =>{ "message" => "%{COMBINEDAPACHELOG}" }
```

```
    }
}
output {
elasticsearch {
        action => "index"
        hosts => ["127.0.0.1:9200"]
        index => "apache_logs"
        user =>elastic_username
        password =>your_password
    }
}
```

Once the file is created under the logstash/conf.d directory, we can execute it using the following command:

bin/logstash -f /etc/logstash/conf.d/apache_data.conf

On successful execution of the preceding command, Logstash will create the apache_logs index in Elasticsearch. We can verify the same in Elasticsearch by executing the following command:

curl -XGET "http://localhost:9200/_cat/indices?v"

The preceding command will list all the Elasticsearch indices, and if we can get the apache_logs index in Elasticsearch, it means Logstash has successfully processed the Apache logs. We can see the documents inside the index by executing the following command:

curl -XGET "http://localhost:9200/apache_logs/_search"

We can see the following document:

```
{
        "_index" : "apache_logs",
        "_type" : "_doc",
        "_id" : "-097j2wBDCiVKm3nWGRa",
        "_score" : 1.0,
        "_source" : {
          "auth" : "-",
          "message" : "127.0.0.1 - - [29/Feb/2020:15:05:20 +0530] \"GET
/test/admin.php HTTP/1.1\" 200 2146 \"-\" \"Mozilla/5.0 (X11; Ubuntu;
Linux x86_64; rv:68.0) Gecko/20100101 Firefox/68.0\"",
          "httpversion" : "1.1",
```

```
    "request" : "/test/admin.php",
    "@timestamp" : "2020-02-29T09:35:21.051Z",
    "clientip" : "127.0.0.1",
    "referrer" : "\"-\"",
    "@version" : "1",
    "response" : "200",
    "ident" : "-",
    "verb" : "GET",
    "host" : "KELLGGNLPTP0305",
    "timestamp" : "29/Feb/2020:15:05:20 +0530",
    "bytes" : "2146",
    "type" : "apache_access",
    "path" : "/var/log/apache2/access.log",
    "agent" : "\"Mozilla/5.0 (X11; Ubuntu; Linux x86_64; rv:68.0)
Gecko/20100101 Firefox/68.0\""
    }
  }
```

This way, we can transform unstructured Apache log entry into structured data in Elasticsearch, which can easily be searched, analyzed, and visualized in Kibana. We can configure Logstash to fetch data from other sources and send it to other destinations. Now, let's explore another important component of Elastic Stack—Kibana.

Kibana

Kibana is an open-source tool that can be used to visualize our Elasticsearch data. It provides various features, like Kibana discover can be used to explore the data by selecting the field's name and search or filter it. Using visualization, we can create different types of graphs while in the dashboard, and we can integrate these visualizations to create a meaningful dashboard. APM helps users monitor the application performance. Dev Tools provide us with an interface to execute Elasticsearch queries right from Kibana. Using Stack Monitoring, we can keep an eye on Elastic Stack performance, and Canvas can be used to apply our creativity to present the data. Using the Timeline, we can play with time-series data and create complex visualizations. Machine learning helps us identify data anomalies and predict future trends, and Kibana SIEM provides a security analytics feature to investigate any possible threat, gather evidence, and forward them to the ticketing system. Using uptime, we can monitor the services to check whether they are up and running. This way, Kibana interface provided us with a whole lot of features to analyze the data.

We can access Kibana on port 5601 after installing it, so we must open the following URL to open Kibana:

http://localhost:5601

If security is enabled, we would get the login screen of Kibana. Refer to the following screenshot:

Figure 3.5: Kibana login screen.

After logging in, we can see different options grouped in different categories, as follows:

- **Observability:** The observability option provides us with the tools to observe the application, logs, and metrics, and so on. Under observability, we can see the APM, logs, and metrics options.

- **Security:** Kibana security enables us to implement the security setup for identifying any possible threat. Under Kibana Security, we have the SIEM tool.

- **Visualize and Explore data:** Under this category, we can see the tool that we can use for data visualization and exploration. Under Visualize and Exploredata, we have APM, Canvas, Dashboard, Discover, Graph, Logs, Machine Learning, Maps, Metrics, SIEM, Uptime, and Visualize.

- **Manage and Administer the Elastic Stack:** This section shows the tools to manage and administer the Elastic Stack. The tools available under this category are Console, Index Patterns, Monitoring, Rollups, Saved Objects, Security Settings, Spaces, and Watchers.

The following screenshot illustrates the Kibana home screen:

Figure 3.6: *Kibana home page*

The preceding screenshot shows the Kibana home page, which lists important tools and the categories they belong to. We can pick a tool based on the type of requirement and use case.

Beats

Beats are single-purpose, lightweight data shippers that can be configured on a machine to fetch data. They can be used to send data from single or thousands of machines to Logstash or directly to Elasticsearch.

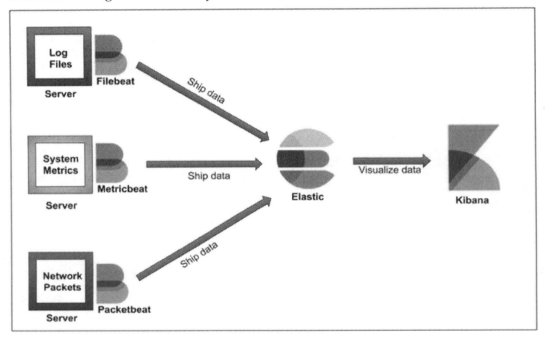

Figure 3.7: Elastic Beats

The preceding diagram shows three different Beats: **Filebeat, Metricbeat**, and **Packetbeat**. These are shipping log file data, system metrics, and network packet data to Elasticsearch, from where Kibana uses that data for visualization. The Beats installation is out of the scope of this book, but you can refer to elastic documentation for the same. Elastic provides the following Beats:

Filebeat

Filebeat is a lightweight data shipper that can be configured to read data from different files. We can ship logs and other data using Filebeat. You can refer to the preceding image, where Filebeat is reading the data from log files and shipping it to the Elasticsearch cluster. Using Filebeat, we can read any file by just providing the directory path in the Filebeat configuration file.

Configure input

We can configure the log input in Filebeat using the `filebeat.yml` file. For this, we need to do the following configurations:

```
filebeat.inputs:
- type: log
  paths:
    - /var/log/messages
    - /var/log/*.log
```

In the preceding code block, we are defining the filebeat inputs section where the type is a log. Under paths, we are defining the messages and all log files under the `/var/log/` directory using a wildcard * so that Filebeat can read all the log files of the given directory. Apart from logs, we can put Stdin, Kafka, UDP, TCP, S3, Syslog, and so on for the input.

Configure output

Filebeat can write to a single specific output source that we can configure using the output section of Filebeat in the filebeat.yml file. Filebeat supports the following output sources:

Elasticsearch

For elasticsearch output, we must configure the `output.elasticsearch` block with the hostname. We can also provide a custom index name if we want to overwrite the default Filebeat index name. Refer to the following code snippet:

```
output.elasticsearch:
  hosts: ["https://localhost:9200"]
  index: "filebeat-%{[agent.version]}-%{+yyyy.MM.dd}"
```

If Elasticsearch is secure, we also need to mention the username and password.

Logstash

If we want the data to be processed before indexing it to Elasticsearch, we can send Filebeat data to Logstash. Using the Logstash output of Filebeat, we can send the Filebeat data to Logstash, and data travels through lumberjack protocol that runs over TCP. We have to configure the **output.logstash** section by providing the host details, as in the following code snippet:

```
output.logstash:
  hosts: ["127.0.0.1:5044"]
```

If there is more than one Logstash host, we can load balance the output, as shown in the following code snippet:

```
output.logstash:
  hosts: ["localhost:5044", "localhost:5045"]
loadbalance: true
  index: filebeat
```

Elastic Cloud

We must configure the elastic cloud section to send the events on Elastic Cloud, as illustrated in the following code snippet:

```
cloud.id: "staging:dXMtZWFzdC0xLmF3er5mb3VuZC5reyRjZWM2ZjI2MWE3NGJnMjRj
ZTMzYmI4ODExYjg0Mjk0ZiRjNmMyY2E2ZDA0MjI0OWFmMGNjN2Q3YTllOTYyNTc0Mw=="
```

```
cloud.auth: "elastic:your_password"
```

Redis

Using the Redis output option, we can push the events to Redis. We must do the following configuration for sending data to Redis:

```
output.redis:
  hosts: ["localhost"]
  password: "your_password"
  key: "filebeat"
db: 0
  timeout: 5
```

File

Using file output, we can push the events to a file in the JSON format. For file output, we need to configure the output.file section using the following code snippet:

```
output.file:
  path: "/tmp/filebeat"
  filename: filebeat
```

We can configure Filebeat to dump data to a file with this code.

Kafka

We can configure the Kafka output section for sending Filebeat data to Apache Kafka. Take a look at the following code snippet to configure the output.kafka section for this:

```
output.kafka:

  # initial brokers for reading cluster metadata

  hosts: ["host1_kafka:9092", "host2_kafka:9092", "host3_kafka:9092"]

  # message topic selection + partitioning

  topic: '%{[fields.topic_name]}'

partition.round_robin:

reachable_only: false

required_acks: 1

  compression: gzip

max_message_bytes: 180000
```

Using the preceding code block, we can configure the Kafka server hosts and topic on which we want to send the message.

Console

Using the console output, we can write data to the standard output in JSON format. To configure the `output.console` section, we must write the following code snippet in the **filebeat.yml** file:

```
output.console:

  pretty: true
```

This way, we can output the Filebeat output to Elasticsearch, Elastic Cloud, Logstash, Redis, File, Kafka, or Console.

Metricbeat

We can fetch metric data from a system using Metricbeat, a lightweight shipper for metric data. The preceding diagram shows that Metricbeat is configured on a server where it is shipping the system metrics to the centralized Elasticsearch cluster. Metricbeat provides important system metrics details, such as CPU usage, memory usage, and availability of disk space.

Configure Metricbeat

We can configure the Metricbeat using the `metricbeat.yml` configuration file, which contains different options to play around.

Enabling the required modules

Metricbeat uses modules to fetch metrics from different services, and we must enable the module for service if we want to collect the metrics of that service. We can enable the modules using the configuration file or through command. For example, if we want to enable the MySQL module of Metricbeat, we can execute the following command for Debian or RPM-based machines:

```
metricbeat modules enable mysql
```

We can enable the MySQL module using the preceding command, and we can similarly enable other modules as well, such as Apache, Nginx, and so on.

Output configuration

We can send Metricbeat data to Elasticsearch or Logstash, or we can configure the Kibana dashboard directly using Metricbeat. If we want to send metrics to Elasticsearch, we can add the following code snippet in the configuration file:

```
output.elasticsearch:
  hosts: ["myEShost:9200"]
```

In the case of Elastic Service, we must add the following code block, where we need to provide the cloud ID:

```
cloud.id: "staging:dXMtZWFzdC0xLmF3er5mb3VuZC5reyRjZWM2ZjI2MWE3NGJn
MjRjZTMzYmI4ODExYjg0Mjk0ZiRjNmMyY2E2ZDA0MjI0OWFmMGNjN2Q3YTllOTYy
NTc0Mw=="
cloud.auth: "elastic:your_password"
```

If we want to send the metrics data to Logstash from Metricbeat, we need to add the following code snippet:

```
output.logstash:
  hosts: ["127.0.0.1:5044"]
```

If we want to configure the sample dashboard of Metricbeat in Kibana, we must provide the Kibana endpoint in the Metricbeat configuration file. This can be done using the following code snippet:

```
setup.kibana:
  host: "localhost:5601"
```

You can mention the IP or URL of your Kibana setup instead of the localhost. This way, we can configure Metricbeat to send metric data from different machines and output the Metricbeat output to Elasticsearch, Elastic Cloud, or Logstash.

Packetbeat

Packetbeat is a lightweight data shipper, using which we can capture the network data. In the preceding diagram, Packetbeat is configured on a server, from where it is shipping the network packet details to the Elasticsearch cluster. Kibana uses the Beats data to create the dashboards and so on.

Configuring Packetbeat

We can configure Packetbeat by editing the packetbeat.yml configuration file. The first thing we need to configure in Packetbeat is the network interface, using which we can capture the traffic. For that, we must configure the `packetbeat.interfaces.device` setting. If we want to capture from all sources, we can configure the following:

```
packetbeat.interfaces.device: any
```

After configuring the interface, we must configure the protocols to monitor. The standard protocols are already given in the configuration file, and we need to add in the configuration file explicitly if we want to monitor any non-standard ports. The following is the configuration file snippet showing some of the protocols and their ports:

```
#=========== Transaction protocols  ==================
packetbeat.protocols:
- type: icmp
  # Enable ICMPv4 and ICMPv6 monitoring. Default: false
  enabled: true
- type: amqp
  # Configure the ports where to listen for AMQP traffic. You can disable
  # the AMQP protocol by commenting out the list of ports.
  ports: [5672]
- type: cassandra
  #Cassandra port for traffic monitoring.
  ports: [9042]
- type: dhcpv4
  # Configure the DHCP for IPv4 ports.
  ports: [67, 68]
- type: dns
  # Configure the ports where to listen for DNS traffic. You can disable
  # the DNS protocol by commenting out the list of ports.
  ports: [53]
- type: http
  # Configure the ports where to listen for HTTP traffic. You can disable
  # the HTTP protocol by commenting out the list of ports.
  ports: [80, 8080, 8000, 5000, 8002]
```

The preceding block shows the protocol and the ports for the protocol.

We can send the Packetbeat data to Logstash or directly to Elasticsearch. We can configure the cloud ID if we want to send the data to Elastic Cloud. Refer to the following code snippet:

```
cloud.id: "staging:dXMtZWFzdC0xLmF3er5mb3VuZC5reyRjZWM2ZjI2MWE3NGJnMjR
jZTMzYmI4ODExYjg0Mjk0ZiRjNmMyY2E2ZDA0MjI0OWFmMGNjN2Q3YTllOTYyNTc0Mw=="
```

```
cloud.auth: "elastic:your_password"
```

If we want to send data to Elasticsearch, which is installed on the hardware or cloud, we can push data using the following code snippet:

```
output.elasticsearch:
  hosts: ["localhost:9200"]
```

If we want to send data to Logstash, we need to add the following code snippet in the configuration file:

```
output.logstash:
  hosts: ["127.0.0.1:5044"]
```

If we want to configure the sample dashboard of Packetbeat, we have to mention the Kibana endpoint in the configuration file, as shown here:

```
setup.kibana:
  host: "localhost:5601"
```

This way, we can output the Packetbeat output to Elasticsearch, Elastic Cloud, or Logstash.

Winlogbeat

Using this data shipper, we can capture the Windows event logs and keep an eye on Windows-based infrastructure to know what is happening there. Winlogbeat helps us stream Windows event logs to Logstash and Elasticsearch.

Configure Winlogbeat

We can configure Winlogbeat by editing the `winlogbeat.yml` configuration file. In the event section of the configuration file, we must specify the events we want to monitor, as illustrated in the following code snippet:

```
winlogbeat.event_logs:
  - name: Application
  - name: System
  - name: Security
```

We can send the Winlogbeat data to Logstash or directly to Elasticsearch. We can configure the cloud ID if we want to send the data to Elastic Cloud, as shown in the following code snippet:

```
cloud.id: "staging:dXMtZWFzdC0xLmF3er5mb3VuZC5reyRjZWM2ZjI2MWE3NGJnMjR
jZTMzYmI4ODExYjg0Mjk0ZiRjNmMyY2E2ZDA0MjI0OWFmMGNjN2Q3YTllOTYyNTc0Mw=="
cloud.auth: "elastic:your_password"
```

If we want to send data to Elasticsearch, which is installed on the hardware or cloud, we can push data using the following code snippet:

```
output.elasticsearch:
  hosts: ["localhost:9200"]
```

If we want to send data to Logstash, we need to add the following code snippet in the configuration file:

```
output.logstash:
  hosts: ["127.0.0.1:5044"]
```

If we want to configure the sample dashboard of Winlogbeat, we have to mention the Kibana endpoint in the configuration file, as shown here:

```
setup.kibana:
  host: "localhost:5601"
```

This way, we can output the Winlogbeat output to Elasticsearch, Elastic Cloud, or Logstash.

Auditbeat

Auditbeat is a lightweight data shipper that sends audit data from Linux machines. Using Auditbeat, we can keep an eye on Linux-based systems, and it helps us monitor processes, user activities, and so on. Auditbeat works as auditd, where it communicates with the Linux audit framework, collects data, and pushes the events directly to Elasticsearch or via Logstash.

Configuring Auditbeat

First, we must enable the modules from where we want to collect the audits. The following code block shows the system module:

```
- module: system
  datasets:
    - host      # General host information, e.g. uptime, IPs
    - login     # User logins, logouts, and system boots.
    - package   # Installed, updated, and removed packages
```

```
- process   # Started and stopped processes
- socket    # Opened and closed sockets
- user      # User information
```

This code shows the default configuration of the module; if we want to add or remove anything, it has to be done in the configuration file.

We can send the Auditbeat data to Logstash or directly to Elasticsearch. We can configure the cloud ID if we want to send the data to Elastic Cloud. Refer to the following code snippet:

```
cloud.id: "staging:dXMtZWFzdC0xLmF3er5mb3VuZC5reyRjZWM2ZjI2MWE3NGJnMjRj
ZTMzYmI4ODExYjg0Mjk0ZiRjNmMyY2E2ZDA0MjI0OWFmMGNjN2Q3YTllOTYyNTc0Mw=="
```

```
cloud.auth: "elastic:your_password"
```

If we want to send data to Elasticsearch, which is installed on the hardware or cloud, we can push it using the following code snippet:

```
output.elasticsearch:
  hosts: ["localhost:9200"]
```

If we want to send data to Logstash, we need to add the following code snippet in the configuration file:

```
output.logstash:
  hosts: ["127.0.0.1:5044"]
```

If we want to configure the sample dashboard of Auditbeat, we must mention the Kibana endpoint in the configuration file, as shown here:

```
setup.kibana:
  host: "localhost:5601"
```

This way, we can output the Auditbeat output to Elasticsearch, Elastic Cloud, or Logstash.

Heartbeat

We use Heartbeat for uptime monitoring; it can monitor the services if they are up and running. Elastic Heartbeat provides a dedicated Uptime screen where we can monitor the service or configure the Kibana Dashboard to monitor the Heartbeat data. It can monitor any service across the web. Heartbeat uses ICMP, TCP, and HTTP protocol to ping, and it also supports TLS.

Configuring Heartbeat

We can configure Heartbeat by editing the `heartbeat.yml` configuration file. For example, if we want to monitor the HTTP service using Heartbeat, we can configure the following code snippet:

```
# /path/to/my/monitors.d/localhost_service_check.yml
- type: http
  schedule: '@every 30s'
  hosts: ["http://localhost:80/servicename/statusendpoint"]
check.response.status: 200
```

Using the preceding code, we can check the service using service hosts every 30 seconds, which can be changed using the schedule and will check the status 200, which is defined for the `check.response.status` field.

Similarly, we can monitor the TCP port using the following code snippet:

```
- type: tcp
  schedule: '@every 10s'
  hosts: ["hostname"]
  ports: [80, 9200, 5044]
```

In the preceding example, we are monitoring ports **80, 9200** and **5044**.

We can send the Heartbeat output to the following:

- Elasticsearch
- Logstash
- Elastic Cloud
- Redis
- File
- Kafka
- Console

If we want to send data to Elasticsearch, which is installed on the hardware or cloud infrastructure, we can push it using the following code snippet:

```
output.elasticsearch:
  hosts: ["localhost:9200"]
```

In the case of Elastic Service, we must add the following code block where we need to provide the cloud ID:

```
cloud.id: "staging:dXMtZWFzdC0xLmF3er5mb3VuZC5reyRjZWM2ZjI2MWE3NGJnMjRj
ZTMzYmI4ODExYjg0Mjk0ZiRjNmMyY2E2ZDA0MjI0OWFmMGNjN2Q3YTllOTYyNTc0Mw=="
```

```
cloud.auth: "elastic:your_password"
```

If we want to send data to Logstash, we need to add the following code snippet in the configuration file:

```
output.logstash:
  hosts: ["127.0.0.1:5044"]
```

This way, we can output the Heartbeat output to Elasticsearch, Elastic Cloud, or Logstash. We are not discussing the other output options of Heartbeat here, but you can refer to the Filebeat configuration section for more information.

Functionbeat

Functionbeat is a Beat for serverless architecture, wherein we can receive data using this Beat. Functionbeat can be deployed as a function on the **Function-as-a-Service (FaaS)** platform for the cloud provider. Once deployed, it will start collecting and shipping data to Elasticsearch. Once the data is pushed on Elasticsearch, we can analyze it.

Configuring Functionbeat

We have to specify the cloud services we want to monitor using Functionbeat. For example, if we want to capture the Cloudwatch events from AWS, we must perform the following configuration:

```
functionbeat.provider.aws.endpoint: "s3.amazonaws.com"
```

```
functionbeat.provider.aws.deploy_bucket: "unique_bucket_name"
```

```
functionbeat.provider.aws.functions:
  - name: name_of_function
    enabled: true
    type: cloudwatch_logs
    description: "lambda function to capture the cloudwatch logs"
    triggers:
      - log_group_name: /aws/lambda/my-lambda-function
```

This way, we can deploy the function on S3 to capture the CloudWatch logs.

We can deploy Functionbeat on the cloud of any provider, such as AWS, Google, and so on. For example, if we want to deploy it on AWS using Linux or Mac environment, we must write the following code:

```
export AWS_ACCESS_KEY_ID=aws_access_key_id
```

```
export AWS_SECRET_ACCESS_KEY=aws_secret_access_key
export AWS_DEFAULT_REGION=aws_region
```

Here, we are configuring the environment variable for AWS. Now, we can execute the following command to deploy Functionbeat:

```
./functionbeat -v -e -d "*" deploy cloudwatch
```

We can configure other settings and output in the same way as we did for other Beats.

We can configure the cloud ID if we want to send the data to Elastic Cloud; refer to the following code snippet:

```
cloud.id:
"staging:dXMtZWFzdC0xLmF3er5mb3VuZC5reyRjZWM2ZjI2MWE3NGJnMjRjZTMzYmI4O
DExYjg0Mjk0ZiRjNmMyY2E2ZDA0MjI0OWFmMGNjN2Q3YTllOTYyNTc0Mw=="
```

```
cloud.auth: "elastic:your_password"
```

We can also configure the Elastic Cloud output using the following command:

```
functionbeat -e -E cloud.id="<cloud-id>" -E cloud.auth="<cloud.auth>"
```

If we want to send data to Elasticsearch, which is installed on the hardware or cloud infrastructure, we can push data using the following code:

```
output.elasticsearch:
  hosts: ["localhost:9200"]
```

If we want to send data to Logstash, we need to add the following code snippet in the configuration file:

```
output.logstash:
  hosts: ["127.0.0.1:5044"]
```

This way, we can output the Functionbeat output to Elasticsearch, Elastic Cloud, or Logstash.

Conclusion

This chapter introduced us to Elastic Stack and its different components. Then, we elaborated on components such as Elasticsearch, Logstash, Kibana, and Beats. After that, we covered how these components work together for different use cases and looked at how we can configure Beats or Logstash to push data into Elasticsearch and then using Kibana; we can create the data visualization.

The next chapter will walk you through how to prepare your data, explain why data preparation is important, and help you understand what Elasticsearch analyzers are.

Questions

1. What is Elastic Stack?

2. What are the different components of the Elastic Stack?

3. What is Logstash, and why do we use it?

4. What are Logstash plugins, and which are the different plugins of Logstash?

5. Create a Logstash configuration file and fetch the log files data.

6. Configure Filebeat to fetch the Apache log data.

CHAPTER 4
Preparing Your Data

Introduction

In the last chapter, we covered the Elastic Stack and explained its different components, such as Elasticsearch, Logstash, Kibana, and different Beats. We also discussed how to configure different Beats for pushing data to Logstash or Elasticsearch. In this chapter, we will cover how to prepare data before indexing. Here, we will look at what data analysis is and how to decide the suitable analysis for the data. Moving on, we will cover different types of analyzers, normalizers, tokenizers, token filters and, character filters in Elasticsearch.

Structure

In this chapter, we will cover the following topics:

- Why it is important to prepare the data before indexing
- Introduction to Elasticsearch Analyzers
- Tokenizers
- Token filters
- Character filters
- Normalizers

Objectives

After studying this unit, you should know:

- What data preparation is
- Elasticsearch analyzers
- Normalizers, tokenizers, token filters, and character filters

Why it is Important to prepare the data before indexing

As the data we store is growing exponentially, it isn't easy to fetch anything specific from the dataset. When we talk about searching, it doesn't mean searching for the exact match. The search criteria can be slightly different than the actual saved data; it may be because of a typo or the use of a synonym or phonetic word where the spelling is different. In any of these situations, we should plan before actually indexing the data. We should know what the use case is and up to what extent we should support the data search. This means if we want to apply a fuzzy search, synonym search, or phonetic search, we can achieve it by just stemming the word for the search. In some cases, we don't want to miss any cases and want to show the results to the end-user even if they type a wrong word.

An introduction to Elasticsearch analyzers

Analyzers are special algorithms that decide how a string field value is transformed into the terms and stored in the form of an inverted index. There are different types of analyzers, and their logic to parse a text is quite different from the other one. Picking the right analyzer for a use case is an art, as there are different use cases for different scenarios. An Elasticsearch analyzer is a combination of character filter, tokenizer, and token filter. Take a look at the following diagram:

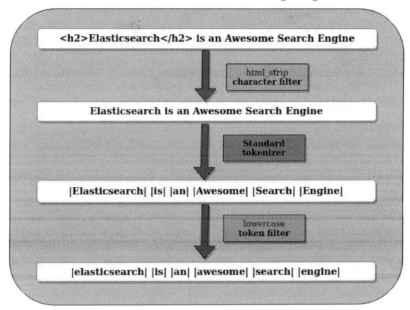

Figure 4.1: *Elasticsearch analyzer*

Here, we can see how the character filter, tokenizer, and token filter work together to achieve the purpose of the analyzer. In the diagram, we have a text saying **Elasticsearch is an Awesome Search Engine**, where we initially have the <h2> tags. At the first level, the html_strip character filter removes the <h2> tags from the text. After that, the Standard tokenizer works and converts the sentence into individual tokens. At last, the lowercase token filter converts the tokens into lowercase tokens. This way, the analyzer converts a sentence into lowercase tokens.

We have many analyzers that come as default analyzers along with the Elasticsearch build. If we want to configure the custom analyzers, it can be done using the setting API of Elasticsearch. The following code snippet shows the configuration of the custom analyzer:

```
PUT /index-name/_settings
{
  "index": {
    "analysis": {
      "analyzer": {
        "customHTMLSnowball": {
          "type": "custom",
```

```
      "char_filter": [
        "html_strip"
      ],
      "tokenizer": "standard",
      "filter": [
        "lowercase",
        "stop",
        "snowball"
      ]
    }
  }
}
}
```

In the preceding code block, we are doing the following:

- We use the `html_strip` character filter to remove all HTML tags from the source text.
- We break the words and remove the punctuation using the standard tokenizer.
- Then, we use the token filters, where the first one is lowercase to convert all tokens to lowercase.
- After that, we have a stop token filter to remove all stop words like the, and, etc.
- At last, we have the snowball token filter, using which we can stem all the tokens.

This way, we can apply a custom analyzer in Elasticsearch using the settings API.

We can specify the analyzer on any field using the following code snippet:

```
PUT /index_name
{
  "mappings": {
    "properties": {
      "text": {
        "type": "text",
        "fields": {
```

```
            "english": {
               "type":        "text",
               "analyzer": "english"
            }
         }
      }
   }
}
```

In the preceding code, the text field uses the default standard analyzer. We are applying the English analyzer on the field level, which applies the stemming and removes the stop words. Using `the_analyze` endpoint, we can see how the analysis is working. Refer to the following example:

```
GET index_name2/_analyze

{
   "field": "text",
   "text": "Elasticsearch is an awesome search engine"
}
```

We are using the text field in the preceding code, and it will provide the following output:

```
{
   "tokens" : [
      {
         "token" : "elasticsearch",
         "start_offset" : 0,
         "end_offset" : 13,
         "type" : "<ALPHANUM>",
         "position" : 0
      },
      {
         "token" : "is",
         "start_offset" : 14,
         "end_offset" : 16,
         "type" : "<ALPHANUM>",
```

```
      "position" : 1
    },
    {
      "token" : "an",
      "start_offset" : 17,
      "end_offset" : 19,
      "type" : "<ALPHANUM>",
      "position" : 2
    },
    {
      "token" : "awesome",
      "start_offset" : 20,
      "end_offset" : 27,
      "type" : "<ALPHANUM>",
      "position" : 3
    },
    {
      "token" : "search",
      "start_offset" : 28,
      "end_offset" : 34,
      "type" : "<ALPHANUM>",
      "position" : 4
    },
    {
      "token" : "engine",
      "start_offset" : 35,
      "end_offset" : 41,
      "type" : "<ALPHANUM>",
      "position" : 5
    }
  ]
}
```

We can also check how the analyzer works for the `text.english` field using the following code:

```
GET index_name2/_analyze
{
  "field": "text.english",
  "text": "Elasticsearch is an awesome search engine"
}
```

The preceding code will provide the following result:

```
{
  "tokens" : [
    {
      "token" : "elasticsearch",
      "start_offset" : 0,
      "end_offset" : 13,
      "type" : "<ALPHANUM>",
      "position" : 0
    },
    {
      "token" : "awesom",
      "start_offset" : 20,
      "end_offset" : 27,
      "type" : "<ALPHANUM>",
      "position" : 3
    },
    {
      "token" : "search",
      "start_offset" : 28,
      "end_offset" : 34,
      "type" : "<ALPHANUM>",
      "position" : 4
    },
    {
      "token" : "engin",
```

```
        "start_offset" : 35,
        "end_offset" : 41,
        "type" : "<ALPHANUM>",
        "position" : 5
    }
  ]
}
```

Here, we can see the stop words are removed, and words have been stemmed.

Built-in analyzer

There are many built-in analyzers that ship with Elasticsearch, and we can use these analyzers directly without any further configuration. Now, let's discuss each of them in detail.

Standard analyzer

The standard analyzer is used by default when we do not specify an analyzer. It uses the Unicode Text Segmentation algorithm, which is based on grammar, to tokenize the sentences. The following code snippet shows the standard analyzer:

```
POST _analyze
{
"analyzer": "standard",
"text": "Elasticsearch is an awesome search engine"
}
```

The preceding code will return the following tokens:

```
[elasticsearch, is, an, awesome, search, engine]
```

It accepts the following parameters:

- `max_token_length`: It denotes the maximum token length. If we provide this length, the analyzer will split tokens with the length provided against the `max_token_length` value. The default value of `max_token_length` is 255 characters.
- `stopwords`: Here, we can specify the `stopwords`, and we can use `the_ english` to specify pre-defined stop words. We can also specify an array list of stop words. By `default _none_` stopword is specified.
- `stopword_path`: Here, we can specify the file path containing stop words.

So, we can use the preceding parameters along with the analyze query to tune the analysis process further.

Simple analyzer

A simple analyzer creates tokens for every non-letter term; it can be space or any other character. We cannot configure the simple analyzer as it only contains a lowercase tokenizer.

The following code snippet shows the simple analyzer and how it breaks the tokens:

```
POST _analyze
{
  "analyzer": "simple",
  "text": "Elasticsearch, is an awesome search engine!"
}
```

The preceding code will generate the following tokens:

`[elasticsearch, is, an, awesome, search, engine]`

This way, it will break the word into tokens if it encounters any special character in between the word.

Whitespace analyzer

The whitespace analyzer converts the text into terms using the `whitespace` character. Whitespace analyzer does not convert the terms into lowercase:

```
POST _analyze
{
  "analyzer": "whitespace",
  "text": "Elasticsearch, is an awesome search engine!"
}
```

The above query will create the following terms:

`[Elasticsearch, is, an, awesome, search, engine!]`

In the preceding terms, we can see that the word "Elasticsearch" is not converted to lowercase.

Stop analyzer

The stop analyzer is quite similar to the simple analyzer, with an additional feature to remove the stop words from the terms. Take a look at the following example, where we are applying the stop analyzer on the same text:

```
POST _analyze
{
  "analyzer": "stop",
  "text": "Elasticsearch, is an awesome search engine!"
}
```

The preceding code will generate the following terms:

[elasticsearch, awesome, search, engine]

Here, we can see that the stop analyzer has also removed the stop words is and a from the terms.

Keyword analyzer

The keyword analyzer returns a single token of the complete set of the input string. The following example shows how the keyword analyzer creates the terms:

```
POST _analyze
{
  "analyzer": "keyword",
  "text": "Elasticsearch, is an awesome search engine!"
}
```

After the execution of the preceding code, we can see the following terms:

[Elasticsearch, is an awesome search engine!]

This way, a single term is generated using the preceding string.

Pattern analyzer

The pattern analyzer splits the text into terms using the regular expression. It also supports the stop words and converts the terms into lower case.

The following code shows how we can create a `pattern` analyzer by providing a non-word pattern:

```
PUT my_index2
{
  "settings": {
    "analysis": {
      "analyzer": {
        "my_email_analyzer": {
```

```
      "type":       "pattern",
      "pattern":    "\\W|_",
      "lowercase": true
    }
   }
  }
 }
}
```

After creating the analyzer, we can apply it with the string. Refer to the following code snippet:

```
POST my_index2/_analyze
{
  "analyzer": "my_email_analyzer",
  "text": "anurag.srivastava@yopmail.com"
}
```

This code will output the following terms:

[anurag, srivastava, yopmail, com]

This way, we can create the pattern to match and convert the string into terms.

Language analyzers

The language analyzer creates terms for specific language text. There are many supported languages, like Arabic, Bengali, Czech, Danish, Dutch, English, Finnish, French, German, Greek, Hindi, Swedish, and so on.

For example, we can apply the English analyzer as a custom analyzer:

```
PUT /english_index
{
  "settings": {
    "analysis": {
      "filter": {
        "english_stop": {
          "type":       "stop",
          "stopwords": "_english_"
        },
```

```
        "english_keywords": {
          "type":         "keyword_marker",
          "keywords":     ["example"]
        },
        "english_stemmer": {
          "type":         "stemmer",
          "language":     "english"
        },
        "english_possessive_stemmer": {
          "type":         "stemmer",
          "language":     "possessive_english"
        }
      },
      "analyzer": {
        "rebuilt_english": {
          "tokenizer":   "standard",
          "filter": [
            "english_possessive_stemmer",
            "lowercase",
            "english_stop",
            "english_keywords",
            "english_stemmer"
          ]
        }
      }
    }
  }
}
```

We can apply any other language analyzer similarly.

Fingerprint analyzer

The fingerprint analyzer uses a fingerprinting algorithm for creating clusters. It converts the text into lowercase, removes extended characters, deduplicates and concatenates the words into a single token. Stop words will be removed if the query is configured with the fingerprint analyzer.

The following code shows the fingerprint analyzer:

```
POST _analyze
{
  "analyzer": "fingerprint",
  "text": "Elasticsearch, is an awesome search engine! awesome"
}
```

The preceding code will generate the following keyword:

```
[an awesome elasticsearch engine is search]
```

The preceding keyword shows a single term that's generated after deduplicating the text.

Custom analyzer

If a built-in analyzer is unsuitable, we can use the custom analyzers. We can combine different character filters, tokenizers, and token filters in a custom analyzer, so we can tweak the tokenizer and filters as per the requirement. Every custom analyzer is a combination of the following:

- A tokenizer
- Zero or more character filters
- Zero or more token filters

Tokenizers

Tokenizers receives a stream of characters from a string and convert it to individual words known as **tokens**. Tokenizers also keep track of the order of each term with the start and end of character offset.

Word oriented tokenizers

Now, we will discuss the tokenizers used to tokenize full text using individual words.

Standard tokenizer

The Standard tokenizer uses the Unicode Text Segmentation algorithm to generate grammar-based tokens. It supports different languages. The following code snippet shows the `standard` tokenizer, which is applied to the text:

```
POST _analyze
{
  "tokenizer": "standard",
  "text": "Elasticsearch, is an awesome search engine!"
}
```

After executing the preceding code, we get the following tokens:

[Elasticsearch, is, an, awesome, search, engine]

In the following terms, we can see all the stop words, and the tokens are not converted to a lower case. We can configure max_token_length to set the max size of each token. By default, the value of max_token_length is 255. If we want to configure max_token_length to 6 characters, we can configure it in the following way:

```
PUT my_index
{
  "settings": {
    "analysis": {
      "analyzer": {
        "my_analyzer": {
          "tokenizer": "my_tokenizer"
        }
      },
      "tokenizer": {
        "my_tokenizer": {
          "type": "standard",
          "max_token_length": 6
        }
      }
    }
  }
}
```

We can create the custom **my_analyzer** analyzer using the preceding code. Now, let's use this analyzer to analyze the text. Refer to the following code snippet:

```
POST my_index/_analyze
{
```

```
  "analyzer": "my_analyzer",
  "text": "Elasticsearch, is an awesome search engine!"
}
```

This will generate the following tokens:

```
[Elasti, csearc, h, is, an awesom, e, search, engine]
```

This way, the terms are a maximum of 6 characters long using the `max_token_length` setting.

Letter tokenizer

The letter tokenizer converts text into a token when it encounters a non-letter character.

The following code snippet shows the `letter` tokenizer:

```
POST _analyze
{
  "tokenizer": "letter",
  "text": "Elasticsearch, is an awesome search-engine!"
}
```

After executing the preceding code, we would get the following tokens:

```
[Elasticsearch, is, an, awesome, search, engine]
```

We can get the preceding tokens using the letter tokenizer. It is not configurable.

Lowercase tokenizer

The lowercase tokenizer is quite similar to the letter tokenizer as it converts text into token whenever it encounters any not-letter character. The only difference is that the lowercase tokenizer converts the tokens into lowercase too. Let's take the same example and try to apply the lowercase tokenizer this time:

```
POST _analyze
{
  "tokenizer": "lowercase",
  "text": "Elasticsearch, is an awesome search-engine!"
}
```

After executing the preceding code, we would get the following tokens:

```
[elasticsearch, is, an, awesome, search, engine]
```

Whitespace tokenizer

The whitespace tokenizer converts text into terms using the whitespace characters. So, text is broken into a term whenever there is a whitespace character. Look at the following code snippet, where we are analyzing the test using the whitespace tokenizer:

```
POST _analyze
{
  "tokenizer": "whitespace",
  "text": "Elasticsearch, is an awesome search-engine!"
}
```

After executing the preceding code, we get the following tokens:

[Elasticsearch, is, an, awesome, search-engine!]

Here, we can see that the terms are broken using the whitespace characters, so all other characters are still there in these terms. We can customize the whitespace tokenizer by configuring the max_token_length parameter.

UAX URL email tokenizer

The uax_url_email tokenizer is similar to the standard tokenizer with one additional feature, wherein it recognizes URLs and email addresses and puts them as a single token. Take a look at the following code snippet, where we will apply the uax_url_email tokenizer on the given text:

```
POST _analyze
{
  "tokenizer": "uax_url_email",
  "text": "Email me at anurag.srivastava@yopmail.com"
}
```

After executing the preceding code, we can the following tokens:

[Email, me, at, anurag.srivastava@yopmail.com]

In the preceding result, we can see that email address has been converted into a term along with other words. We can customize the uax_url_email tokenizer by configuring the max_token_length parameter.

Classic tokenizer

We can use classic tokenizer for the English Language as it is a grammar-based tokenizer. It understands the email addresses, internet hostnames, and so on, and stores them as a single token. It splits the words using punctuation characters by removing the punctuations. The following code snippet illustrates an example of the `classic` tokenizer:

```
POST _analyze
{
  "tokenizer": "classic",
  "text": "Elasticsearch, is an awesome search-engine!"
}
```

After executing the preceding code, we get the following tokens:
`[Elasticsearch, is, an, awesome, search, engine]`

In the preceding result, we can see that the hyphen is also used to create the terms. We can customize the classic tokenizer by configuring the `max_token_length` parameter.

Partial word tokenizers

We can use partial word tokenizers for a use case where we want to do partial word matching, and the word is broken into small fragments for that.

N-gram tokenizer

N-Gram tokenizer works like a sliding window, where we can slide it on a word. It converts the text into a continuous sequence of characters of the specified length. We can use the sequence for partial word matching where it would be difficult to match the exact word. By default, the `ngram` tokenizer produces N-gram with a minimum length of 1 and a maximum length of 2. The following code snippet illustrates an example of the `ngram` tokenizer.

```
POST _analyze
{
  "tokenizer": "ngram",
  "text": "Elasticsearch"
}
```

We get the following result:
`[E, El, l, la, a, as, s, st, t, ti, i, ic, c, cs, s, se, e, ea, a, ar, r, rc, c, ch, h]`

In the preceding token results, we can see that the word Elasticsearch is converted into single and double character tokens. The `ngram` tokenizer accepts the following parameters:

- min_gram: By default, the minimum length of a character is 1, which we change using this parameter.
- max_gram: By default, the maximum length of characters is 2, which we can set using this parameter.
- token_chars: We can provide the character classes that we want to include in the token.
- custom_token_chars: These are custom characters that should be treated as part of a token.

Using the preceding parameters, we can further tweak the ngram tokenizer's performance.

Edge n-gram tokenizer

The edge_ngram tokenizer is similar to the ngram tokenizer, with the main difference being that the start of the edge_ngram is anchored to the beginning of the word. These are well suited for the search-as-you-type queries. The following code snippet provides an edge_ngram example:

```
POST _analyze
{
  "tokenizer": "edge_ngram",
  "text": "Elasticsearch"
}
```

After executing the preceding code, we get the following output:

```
[E, El]
```

We have the following parameters that we can use to configure:

- min_gram: By default, the minimum length of a character is 1, which we change using this parameter.
- max_gram: By default, the maximum length of characters is 2, which we can set using this parameter.
- token_chars: We can provide the character classes that we want to include in the token.
- custom_token_chars: These are custom characters that should be treated as part of a token.

Structured Text Tokenizers

Instead of full text, we can use the structured text tokenizers when we want to play with structured texts like email addresses, ZIP codes, identifiers, path, and so on.

Keyword tokenizer

The keyword tokenizer accepts the text and outputs the same text as a single term. The following code snippet shows a keyword tokenizer example:

```
POST _analyze
{
  "tokenizer": "keyword",
  "text": "Elasticsearch"
}
```

After executing the preceding code, we will get the following term:

`[Elasticsearch]`

Here, we can see that the same word Elasticsearch is passed to the keyword tokenizer, and the same word is generated as a token.

Pattern tokenizer

The pattern tokenizer splits the text into term using a regular expression. It works the same way as we explained the pattern analyzer. The default pattern is \W+, which splits text whenever it encounters non-word characters.

Token filters

Token filters receive the token streams from the tokenizer and can modify the tokens. These modifications can be to convert text into lowercase, delete tokens, add tokens, and so on. There are many built-in token filters that we can use to build custom analyzers. The token filters include the following features:

- The lowercase token filters convert the received tokenizer text into lowercase tokens.
- The uppercase token filters convert the received tokenizer text into uppercase tokens.
- The stop token filters remove the stop words from the token streams.
- We can reverse the tokens using the reverse token filter.
- We can remove the elisions using the elision token filter.
- We can cut the token into a specific length using the truncate token filter. By default, the length is set to 10.
- We can index the unique tokens using the unique token filter.
- We can remove duplicate tokens that are identical in the same position using the duplicate token filter.

This way, we can use the token filter to achieve the preceding features.

Character filters

Character filters works before the stream of characters are passed to the tokenizer. They process the stream of characters by removing, adding, or modifying the character before passing them to the tokenizer. There are many built-in character filters available in Elasticsearch, using which we can build custom analyzers.

HTML strip character filter

Using the `html_strip` character filter, we can strip the HTML elements from the text and replace HTML entities using their decoded value. The following code snippet illustrates the `html_strip` character filter:

```
POST _analyze
{
  "tokenizer":      "keyword",
  "char_filter":  [ "html_strip" ],
  "text": "<p>I&apos;m so <b>happy</b>!</p>"
}
```

After executing the preceding code, we get the following term:

```
[ \nI'm so happy!\n ]
```

The `html_strip` character filter supports the following parameter:

- `escaped_tags`: Here, we can provide the array of HTML tags that we don't want to be stripped from the original text.

Using the preceding parameter, we can add some HTML tags that we don't want to modify.

Mapping the char filter

Mapping char filters use an associative array with key and their values. In case of a text match with the key, the filter replaces that key with their value. Using this character filter, we can transform a language into any other language. For example, we can easily transform the Hindu-Arabic numerals to Arabic-Latin numbers using the mapping character filter.

Pattern replace character filter

Using the `pattern_replace` character filter, we can replace the characters by applying the regular expression. We can specify the replacement string against the regular expression. The `pattern_replace` character filter supports the following parameters:

- `pattern`: A regular expression in Java.
- `replacement`: The replacement string that can be used to replace the existing string on matching the regular expression.
- `flags`: Pipe separated flags for Java regular expression.

For example "**CASE_INSESSITIVE|COMMENTS**".

We can use the preceding parameters to tweak the character filter's behavior.

Normalizers

Normalizers are quite similar to analyzers, but instead of producing multiple tokens, normalizers produce just one token. Normalizers do not contain tokenizers and accept some of the character filters and token filters. The filters that we can use are `asciifolding`, `cjk_width`, `decimal_digit`, `elision`, `lowercase`, and `uppercase`. Along with these filters, it uses some language filters. We can create a custom normalizer by providing the character filters and token filters. Take a look at the following code snippet:

```
PUT index
{
  "settings": {
    "analysis": {
      "char_filter": {
        "quote": {
          "type": "mapping",
          "mappings": [
            "« => \"",
            "» => \""
          ]
        }
      },
      "normalizer": {
        "my_normalizer": {
          "type": "custom",
          "char_filter": ["quote"],
          "filter": ["lowercase", "asciifolding"]
        }
```

```
        }
      }
    },
  "mappings": {
    "properties": {
      "foo": {
        "type": "keyword",
        "normalizer": "my_normalizer"

      }
    }
  }
}
```

In the preceding example, we are using the `quote` character `filter,` `lowercase` and `asciifolding` filter for the normalizer. This way, we can create the custom normalizer.

Conclusion

In this chapter, we learned what data analysis is and why it is important. We also covered what an analyzer, normalizer, tokenizer, token filter, and character filter are. Then, we looked at the different types of analyzers and where we can use them, before moving on to discussing different normalizers, tokenizers, token filters, and character filters and where to use them.

The next chapter will cover data ingestion, storage, and visualization. We will also understand how to push data into Elasticsearch using different Beats. Additionally, we will explore how Logstash can be configured to fetch data from different sources to send it to Elasticsearch.

Questions

1. What is Elasticsearch analyzer?
2. Explain the built-in analyzer.
3. What is the pattern analyzer?
4. What is the use of tokenizer?
5. What is the use of a token filter?
6. What is the use of a character filter?
7. What is the use of normalizers?

## CHAPTER 5

Importing Data into Elasticsearch

Introduction

In the last chapter, we saw how to prepare the data before indexing, and we learned what data analysis is and how to decide the suitable analysis for the data. Then, we covered different types of analyzers, normalizers, tokenizers, token filters and, character filters in Elasticsearch. In this chapter, we will start with why data is so important for a business, and then we will cover what data ingestion, storage, and visualization are. After that, we will discuss how to import data into Elasticsearch using different Beats, and we will explain how Logstash can be used to import data into Elasticsearch. So, let's start by understanding why data is so important.

Structure

In this chapter, we will cover the following:

- Why is data so important for business?
- Data shipping
- Data ingestion
- Data storage
- Data visualization
- Importing data into Elasticsearch using different Beats

Objectives

After studying this unit, you should be able to:

- Understand the importance of data for a business
- Do the data shipping
- Understand what data ingestion, storage, and visualization are
- Import data using Elastic Beats and Logstash

Why is data so important for business

The right set of information is very much required for any business, and it is hidden behind raw data. We need to process the data to get meaningful information. Data can be of many types, such as time-series data, structured data, or unstructured data, and we need to make it uniform to get meaningful information. Many times, we have data flowing from different sources, and we can get the relationship between these if we process and put the data in a single dashboard. So, we must do the following to get the complete picture:

- Identify the business need.
- Identify all sources of the data required for the business need.
- Transform the data to make it uniform; this includes converting any unstructured data to structured data and covert the field values to make it uniform.
- Ingest data and transform it as per a common schema.
- Store data in a single place.
- Create a unified dashboard for data visualization and analysis.

Using the preceding steps, we can get all integrated information required to understand the business requirement. Once the data is collected in a unified format, we can analyse it to fetch meaningful information that can provide insights to transform the organization. This way, raw data is very important for any business, and many organizations around the world are working on data by analyzing it and collecting meaningful information out of it. They are building alerting and ticketing systems on top of this data for proactive monitoring, and they are also applying machine learning to detect any anomalies and predict future trends. This way, they are preparing for future requirements and improving their processes accordingly.

Data shipping

Data shipping is a process where we ship the data from remote machines to a centralized location. The data shipping architecture should support different types of data or events' transport like structured data or unstructured data. The main purpose of data shipping is to push data to central storage, where we can use it for further exploration. For data shipping, we generally deploy lightweight agents that are basically for a single purpose. These lightweight shippers are installed and configured to read the data on remote servers and ship them to a central place. We must consider the following points for data shipping:

- The lightweight shippers should have a small footprint so that they cannot impact the performance of the actual server processes.

- We have several data shipping tools that support different technologies. Some of them are tied to specific technologies, while others are based on the extensible framework.

- Shipping data also requires security, where we need to send data to the destination from a remote server with an end-to-end secured pipeline.

- We must also understand how the load is handled in data shipping. It should support the load management where the end destination can ingest data, and the shipping speed should be reduced whenever there is an issue at the destination. This feature is known as back-pressure management.

Data shipping is a very important aspect for data analysis, as it is important to fetch data from different sources for data analysis or visualization. For example, if we want to build a centralized log management system, it is important to ship logs from all servers. We can apply the data visualization or analysis only after the data reaches central storage.

Data ingestion

Data ingestion is a process that encompasses a wide range of transport protocols that are commonly used along with different data formats. It provides the capability to extract and transform data before storing it. Data processing is a process where we extract, transform, and load data, and this process is also known as ETL. ETL is also known as an ingestion pipeline, using which we can receive data from different shipping layers, like Beats or Logstash, and push it to the storage layer. Data ingestion has the following features:

- The main purpose of the ingestion layer is to prepare the data, where we parse and format the data, correlate it with other data sources, normalize it, and enrich it before storing it. The ultimate goal is to improve the data quality so that we can analyse it. There are many other advantages of data ingestion, such that the data improvement also helps us remove the additional effort of processing overhead. If data is not in proper shape, we have to do this by applying pre-computation before analysis. For example, there may be certain variations in the data if we fetch it from different sources, and we need to correct these to improve the data quality, apply the analysis, and create different visualizations.

- The ingestion layer supports an architecture where we can have different pluggable modules, which helps us fetch data from different sources and different destinations. We can use these plugins along with the shipper to get specific data from a destination; for example, if we want to fetch data from any file, a network, or from a database, we can use different available plugins that are designed for specific purposes. Sometimes, we can have multiple options to fetch data, and it depends on the use case to pick the right option. For example, we can use various Beats to fetch specific data, and Logstash can also be used to fetch the same data. We should pick Logstash if we want to transform the data, otherwise Beats can be used.

- When we ingest data and transform it, we need a lot of computing resources. So, we need to plan accordingly to maximize the data throughput, like to distribute the load over multiple instances of ingestion. If we want to create a (near) real-time visualization system, it is quite important to ingest data as soon as possible. For that, it is very important to distribute the load among multiple ingestion instances. This way, we can accelerate the storage of data, which can then be used for visualization.

Elastic Beats and Logstash can be used for data ingestion, as they can be configured to push data from any data source. Once the data is in, we can transform it as per the requirement. After transformation, we can push the data to the storage layer, where Elasticsearch can be used to store the data. Once the data is stored in Elasticsearch, we can configure the visualization layer to create different visualization, and we can use Kibana for data visualization. Kibana provides us with a feature to create a different type of visualization, and then we can create the dashboard by integrating different visualizations.

Data storage

In a data-driven architecture, the heart is the data storage because we can apply the analysis only after storing the data. Data storage is a process where we can store the essential data for the long term based on the decided retention period. Storage provides the platform, using which we can apply different functionalities like data search, analysis, and visualization. Ideally, the heart of a data analysis system is storage because we fetch data from different sources and store it to a centralized place, from where we can apply data analysis and visualization. The following points must be considered for data storage:

- As data is growing day by day, we may face issues with storage capacity, as capacity planning is very important, and we have to consider different aspects like the indexing speed of data, the retention period, and so on. Data volumes can vary, like it can differ from gigabytes to terabytes to petabytes. Scalability is an important aspect as it provides us with a feature where we can horizontally scale when the demand and data volume grows by adding additional machines to seamlessly increase storage.

- For data storage, we mostly use a highly distributed non-relational data store. The advantage of using a non-relational and highly distributed data store is its ability to quicken data access, support different data types, and apply analysis on a high volume of data. The data can be partitioned and spread over different machines to distribute the load and balance it for the read and write operation.

- The storage layer should also expose the API so that other layers, like data visualization and data analysis, can use those APIs for further processing. Once the data is stored, the visualization layer can perform statistical analysis on top of it, and it can also aggregate the data. All the heavy lifting is mostly done at storage level, while visualization only uses the data and renders the result.

Data storage is the heart of data processing, and we primarily use Elasticsearch for storing data. Elasticsearch provides us with various features like near real-time data availability, search capabilities, aggregation to aggregate data of any size, and shading to scale Elasticsearch cluster on multiple nodes.

The sharding feature of Elasticsearch helps us horizontally scale Elasticsearch so that we can manage a large scale of data easily. The search capabilities of Elasticsearch make it the best data storage tool, as it is sometimes very difficult to search the relevant term from a huge set of data collection. The aggregation feature of Elasticsearch helps us get an insight into the whole dataset quickly, and any user can get the benefit of data aggregation.

Under the visualization layer, Kibana also takes advantage of the data aggregation feature of Elasticsearch to create various graphs, charts, and so on. Elasticsearch also exposes the REST APIs, using which we can easily perform different operations. Elasticsearch does all the heavy lifting by processing the data so that the visualization layer has to just render the data in visual form instead of any processing. This way, Elasticsearch provides various features on the data storage layer that are required for data processing.

Data visualization

The visualization layer is an important aspect of data analysis, as it provides the window on the data. Data visualization includes a different set of tools, using which we can build graphs and charts. By including meaningful and related graphs and charts, we can create insightful dashboards that can help us answer different questions, like What is happening in the system? Is everything fine? What is the trend? Is there any issue in the system? The main purpose of the visualization layer is to bring all-important KPIs and show them in a meaningful dashboard. Using this dashboard, the management can take decisions for the organization. The visualization layer has the following features:

- The visualization layer should be lightweight and capable of creating visualizations and graphs using the data from the storage layer. All the heavy lifting, such as processing, should be done at the storage layer, and the visualization layer should only render the result.

- It should provide a quick insight into the data by showing all-important KPIs, and it should also provide the option to discover the data.

- Instead of exploring the complete data, the visualization layer provides a visual way to answer the questions.

- The visualization layer should provide the visual data in near real-time so that it can help us solve any issue promptly.

- The visualization framework has to extensible so that we can customize the existing assets, remove them, or add new assets as per the requirement.

- The visualization layer should provide the option to share the dashboard externally so that we can use that in any external application.

- It is always good if the visualization layer can provide some extra features out of the box, like machine learning, using which we can predict future trends or identify any anomaly in the data.

- The visualization layer should also provide the interface, using which we can easily import data instead of using any other tool.

The following diagram shows the different layers and how they are connected:

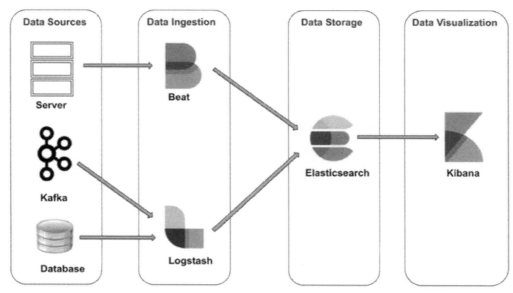

Figure 5.1: Data visualization after fetching it from different sources.

In the preceding diagram, we can see how data is flowing from a data source to the visualization layer through data ingestion and storage. Here, the data source can be a server, Kafka, or any database. At the same time, Beats or Logstash can be used for data ingestion, and data can then be stored in Elasticsearch, which is primarily used for data storage. Once data is in Elasticsearch, Kibana can use it for visualization. This way, data processing is completed through different layers.

Importing data into Elasticsearch using different Beats

Elastic provides different Beats that are lightweight data shippers; we can install and configure them on a remote server to fetch data and store it in the centralized server. Here, we will understand how we can configure some of them to fetch data from the remote server. The following diagram illustrates how we can fetch data using Beats:

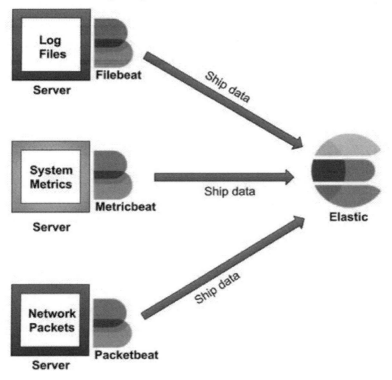

Figure 5.2: Elastic Beats

The preceding diagram shows Filebeat, Metricbeat, and Packetbeat, which are installed and configured on servers. Filebeat is fetching log file data and shipping it to a centralized Elasticsearch cluster. Metricbeat is fetching the system metric data from the server and pushing it to Elasticsearch, while Packetbeat is fetching network packet data and pushing it to Elasticsearch. Now, let's see how we can configure these Beats to push data from remote servers. We have already explored the Beats in an earlier chapter, so we'll now look at how data can be imported using different Beats. Let's start with Filebeat.

Pull Apache logs using Filebeat

Filebeat is a lightweight shipper for the logs, using which we can ship logs to centralized storage. Filebeat supports internal modules for different tools and software such as Apache, NGINX, and MySQL. Using these modules, Filebeat eases down the log collection, parsing, and visualization for these log formats for the supported module. Now, we will cover a scenario where we want to push Apache logs into Elasticsearch using Filebeat. The first step is to check whether Filebeat is working properly. We need to check the service by running the following command on Ubuntu:

```
sudo service filebeat status
```

The preceding command shows the status of Filebeat service; if the service is not running, we would get the following response on terminal:

```
filebeat.service - Filebeat sends log files to Logstash or directly to
Elasticsearch.
   Loaded: loaded (/lib/systemd/system/filebeat.service; disabled; vendor
preset: enabled)
   Active: inactive (dead)
```

In that case, we can start the service by executing the following command:

```
sudo service filebeat start
```

The preceding command will start the Filebeat service and if we try to execute the preceding status command after that, it will provide the following response:

```
filebeat.service - Filebeat sends log files to Logstash or directly to
Elasticsearch.
   Loaded: loaded (/lib/systemd/system/filebeat.service; disabled; vendor
preset: enabled)
   Active: active (running) since Sat 2020-03-28 20:25:48 IST; 3s ago
```

The preceding response denotes that Filebeat is up and running. The following screenshot shows the Filebeat service status:

```
Q                                                              Terminal
user@KELLGGNLPTP0305:~$ sudo service filebeat status
[sudo] password for user:
● filebeat.service - Filebeat sends log files to Logstash or directly to Elasticsearch.
   Loaded: loaded (/lib/systemd/system/filebeat.service; disabled; vendor preset: enabled)
   Active: inactive (dead)
     Docs: https://www.elastic.co/products/beats/filebeat
user@KELLGGNLPTP0305:~$ sudo service filebeat start
user@KELLGGNLPTP0305:~$ sudo service filebeat status
● filebeat.service - Filebeat sends log files to Logstash or directly to Elasticsearch.
   Loaded: loaded (/lib/systemd/system/filebeat.service; disabled; vendor preset: enabled)
   Active: active (running) since Sat 2020-03-28 20:25:48 IST; 3s ago
     Docs: https://www.elastic.co/products/beats/filebeat
 Main PID: 2003 (filebeat)
    Tasks: 14 (limit: 4915)
   Memory: 58.3M
   CGroup: /system.slice/filebeat.service
           └─2003 /usr/share/filebeat/bin/filebeat -e -c /etc/filebeat/filebeat.yml -path.
```

Figure 5.3: Starting the Filebeat service.

The preceding screenshot shows the details of the status check of Filebeat, where the first command is to check the status, which shows that the service is inactive. In the next command, we started the service, and the status is showing that the service is active.

Now, we will configure Filebeat to push the Apache logs from the server to Elasticsearch, where those log details would be stored for further analysis and visualization. The following is the format for Apache 2 log file entry:

```
127.0.0.1 - - [28/Mar/2020:21:09:05 +0530] "GET /test/admin.
php?server=35.175.152.194&username=root HTTP/1.1" 403 4293 "http://
localhost/test/admin.php?server=35.175.152.194&username=root"
"Mozilla/5.0 (X11; Ubuntu; Linux x86_64; rv:72.0) Gecko/20100101
Firefox/72.0"
```

For configuring Filebeat to read the preceding Apache 2 logs, we first need to make the following change in the filebeat.yml Filebeat configuration file:

```
#==================Filebeat inputs ===============

filebeat.inputs:

# Each - is an input. Most options can be set at the input level, so

# you can use different inputs for various configurations.

# Below are the input specific configurations.

- type: log

  # Change to true to enable this input configuration.
```

```
enabled: false


# Paths that should be crawled and fetched. Glob based paths.
paths:
  - /var/log/apache2/*.log
```

In the preceding *Filebeat inputs* section, we need to define the path of the log location. As we want to read the Apache 2 logs, we must provide the path of Apache 2 log location. Also, we have mentioned *.log so that Filebeat can read all log files at the /var/log/apache2/ location. We can configure other locations similarly, or we can provide the path as /var/log/*.log if we want to read all log files inside the log directory. Then, Filebeat will access all log files inside the /var/log/ location.

After setting the log location, we need to configure the Elasticsearch output where we want to send the data, and we must perform the following configuration for that:

```
#================================ Outputs ================================
# Configure what output to use when sending the data collected by the
beat.


#-------------------- Elasticsearch output -------------------------
----
output.elasticsearch:
  # Array of hosts to connect to.
  hosts: ["localhost:9200"]


  # Optional protocol and basic auth credentials.
  #protocol: "https"
  username: "elastic"
  password: "your_password"
```

In the preceding snippet of the filebeat.yml file, we are configuring the Elasticsearch output. Here, we need to provide the host address, protocol, username, and password of Elasticsearch so that Filebeat can connect with Elasticsearch to send the log data. If we want to send data to Logstash instead of sending it directly to Elasticsearch, we must configure the *Logstash output* section by providing the Logstash host details, and so on. If we want to send the log data to the Elastic Cloud, we have to provide the cloud ID under the *Elastic Cloud* section of the filebeat.yml file. From Beats version 6.0.0 onward, the dashboards can be loaded via the Kibana API. For loading the Kibana dashboards, we have to configure the Kibana endpoint in the Filebeat configuration file under the Kibana section. This way, we can configure the Filebeat configuration as per the requirement.

After making these changes, we have to start the Filebeat service. Now we can list all the indices of Elasticsearch to check whether the Filebeat index is created, so we need to execute the following command:

```
curl -XGET "http://localhost:9200/_cat/indices?v"
```

This command will list all the indices, and we can see the filebeat-7.6.1 index. We can overwrite the index name by providing the index name in the Filebeat configuration. Now we can see the index documents by executing the following command:

```
curl -XGET "http://localhost:9200/filebeat-7.6.1/_search"
```

The preceding command will open the index, and we can see all the documents. The document format is as follows:

```
{
        "_index" : "filebeat-7.6.1",
        "_type" : "_doc",
        "_id" : "bc9hInEBi181GZBHM3l8",
        "_score" : 1.0,
        "_source" : {
          "agent" : {
            "hostname" : "KELLGGNLPTP0305",
            "id" : "83179236-86ac-4116-bdea-64b770a8bd49",
            "type" : "filebeat",
            "ephemeral_id" : "22f8ef10-31b5-4429-b1ab-bdb2fedff829",
            "version" : "7.6.1"
          },
          "log" : {
            "file" : {
              "path" : "/var/log/apache2/access.log"
            },
            "offset" : 309145
          },
          "source" : {
            "address" : "127.0.0.1",
```

```
      "ip" : "127.0.0.1"
    },
    "fileset" : {
      "name" : "access"
    },
    "url" : {
      "original" : "/test/admin.php?username=admin"
    },
    "input" : {
      "type" : "log"
    },
    "@timestamp" : "2020-03-28T18:22:02.000Z",
    "ecs" : {
      "version" : "1.4.0"
    },
    "host" : {
      "hostname" : "KELLGGNLPTP0305",
      "os" : {
        "kernel" : "5.0.0-38-generic",
        "codename" : "disco",
        "name" : "Ubuntu",
        "family" : "debian",
        "version" : "19.04 (Disco Dingo)",
        "platform" : "ubuntu"
      }
    },
    "http" : {
      "request" : {
        "referrer" : "http://localhost/test/admin.php",
        "method" : "GET"
      },
      "response" : {
        "status_code" : 403,
```

```
        "body" : {
          "bytes" : 4327
        }
      },
      "version" : "1.1"
    },
    "event" : {
      "created" : "2020-03-28T18:22:05.469Z",
      "module" : "apache",
      "dataset" : "apache.access"
    },
    "user_agent" : {
      "original" : "Mozilla/5.0 (X11; Ubuntu; Linux x86_64;
rv:72.0) Gecko/20100101 Firefox/72.0",
      "os" : {
        "name" : "Ubuntu"
      },
      "name" : "Firefox",
      "device" : {
        "name" : "Other"
      },
      "version" : "72.0."
    }
  }
}
```

This way, we can configure Filebeat to read any log and index in Elasticsearch. Using Filebeat modules, we can read data from other sources, such as MySQL, NGINX, and so on, but that is out of the scope for this book. Our main focus is to explain certain Elastic Stack features for a better understanding of their importance for Elasticsearch.

Pull server metrics using Metricbeat

Metricbeat is a lightweight data shipper that can be configured to a remote server for fetching system metrics such as CPU usage, memory usage, disk IO, network IO, and file system. Also, we can fetch the stats for different processes running on the server. Now, let's see how we can fetch the system metrics using Metricbeat.

After fetching the server metrics, we must install and configure Metricbeat on the server. We have already covered the Beat installation in *Chapter 3, Working with Elastic Stack,* so you can refer to that chapter if you want to understand how to install Metricbeat. After installation, we need to configure Metricbeat by editing the `metricbeat.yml` Metricbeat configuration file. The following code snippet shows the module's configuration, using which we can configure the directory from where we can read the module's configuration file:

```
#=======================  Modules configuration
===========================

metricbeat.config.modules:

  # Glob pattern for configuration loading
  path: ${path.config}/modules.d/*.yml


  # Set to true to enable config reloading
reload.enabled: false


  # Period on which files under path should be checked for changes
  #reload.period: 10s
```

By default, it picks the configuration from the `modules.d` directory, but we can change the location by editing the directory path in the `metricbeat.yml` configuration file.

After the modules setting, we need to configure the Elasticsearch output section. Here, we need to configure the Elasticsearch credentials so that the metric data can be pushed to Elasticsearch. The following code snippet shows the Elasticsearch output section of the `Metricbeat` configuration file:

```
#---------------------- Elasticsearch output --------------------------
output.elasticsearch:
  # Array of hosts to connect to.
  hosts: ["localhost:9200"]


  # Optional protocol and basic auth credentials.
  #protocol: "https"
  username: "elastic"
  password: "your_password"
```

We can configure the Elasticsearch output to send the Metricbeat data in Elasticsearch. In the preceding configuration, we need to provide the protocol, username, password, and host details. After configuring the `metricbeat.yml` file, we have to restart the Metricbeat service using the following command:

```
sudo service metricbeat restart
```

Once the Metricbeat service starts, it will begin fetching the server metrics and send them to the Elasticsearch cluster.

Now, we can list all the indices of Elasticsearch to check whether Filebeat index is created by executing the following command:

```
curl -XGET "http://localhost:9200/_cat/indices?v"
```

The preceding command will list all the indices, and there we can see the `metricbeat-7.6.1` index. We can overwrite the index name by providing the index name in the Metricbeat configuration. We can see the index documents by executing the following command:

```
curl -XGET "http://localhost:9200/metricbeat-7.6.1/_search?
```

The preceding command will open the index, and we can see all the documents. The document format is as follows:

```
{
        "_index" : "metricbeat-7.6.1",
        "_type" : "_doc",
        "_id" : "6tqrK3EBGmw9CiLI4uE4",
        "_score" : 1.0,
        "_source" : {
          "@timestamp" : "2020-03-30T13:40:07.920Z",
          "service" : {
            "type" : "system"
          },
          "system" : {
            "filesystem" : {
              "total" : 11010048,
              "type" : "squashfs",
              "used" : {
                "pct" : 1,
                "bytes" : 11010048
              },
```

```
          "free" : 0,
          "files" : 2475,
          "device_name" : "/dev/loop18",
          "mount_point" : "/snap/landing-team-tools/2",
          "available" : 0,
          "free_files" : 0
      }
  },
  "ecs" : {
    "version" : "1.4.0"
  },
  "host" : {
    "name" : "KELLGGNLPTP0305",
    "architecture" : "x86_64",
    "os" : {
      "platform" : "ubuntu",
      "version" : "19.04 (Disco Dingo)",
      "family" : "debian",
      "name" : "Ubuntu",
      "kernel" : "5.0.0-38-generic",
      "codename" : "disco"
    },
    "id" : "3981136c89ec40e496c3b850831321fe",
    "containerized" : false,
    "hostname" : "KELLGGNLPTP0305"
  },
  "agent" : {
    "version" : "7.6.1",
    "type" : "metricbeat",
    "ephemeral_id" : "4af46a26-ebf6-41e2-97a3-b43ca017973e",
    "hostname" : "KELLGGNLPTP0305",
    "id" : "099136c0-5d5e-4bc1-b5eb-62d3e5ce9515"
  },
```

```
      "event" : {
        "dataset" : "system.filesystem",
        "module" : "system",
        "duration" : 2915077797
      },
      "metricset" : {
        "name" : "filesystem",
        "period" : 60000
      }
    }
  }
```

The Metricbeat index shows different server metrics data like the details of the filesystem, OS, CPU, and memory, and so on. This way, we can configure the Metricbeat to read the system metrics and index that in Elasticsearch. System metrics include different details, like filesystem, OS, CPU, and memory, and so on. We can also configure the pre-defined dashboard in Kibana by configuring it through Metricbeat.

Pulling network data using Packetbeat

Packetbeat is a lightweight data shipper, using which we can monitor the network traffic. It can send the network packet data to Logstash or directly to Elasticsearch. I have already covered the configuration steps in *Chapter 3, Working with Elastic Stack*, but to reiterate, the steps are as follows:

- We need to configure the network interface from which we want to capture the traffic in the `Packetbeat` configuration file.

- Configure the protocol type and port number from where we want to capture the traffic in the `Packetbeat` configuration file.

- Configure the output section where we want to send the data; for example, Logstash, Elasticsearch Cloud, or Elasticsearch Cluster, and so on.

- If we want to create a default Packetbeat dashboard, we also need to provide the Kibana endpoint in the Packetbeat configuration file.

For more detail, refer to *Chapter 3, Working with Elastic Stack*. If we want to know all available interfaces, we need to run the following command:

```
packetbeat devices
```

The preceding command will output the following:

```
user@KELLGGNLPTP0305:/var/log$ packetbeat devices
0: wlo1 (No description available) (192.168.43.127 fe80::d8a9:723a:899d:eff7)
1: any (Pseudo-device that captures on all interfaces) (Not assigned ip address)
2: lo (No description available) (127.0.0.1 ::1)
3: virbr0 (No description available) (192.168.122.1)
4: docker0 (No description available) (172.17.0.1)
5: enp0s25 (No description available) (Not assigned ip address)
6: virbr0-nic (No description available) (Not assigned ip address)
7: nflog (Linux netfilter log (NFLOG) interface) (Not assigned ip address)
8: nfqueue (Linux netfilter queue (NFQUEUE) interface) (Not assigned ip address)
user@KELLGGNLPTP0305:/var/log$ ▮
```

Figure 5.4: Packetbeat devices command output.

In this screenshot, we can see that there are eight interfaces from where we can choose the interface to monitor the network traffic, or we can monitor it from all the interfaces. If we want to monitor the first interface, we can configure it using the following command:

packetbeat.interfaces.device: 0

This way, we can monitor only the first interface. The next thing is to configure the protocols we want to monitor. Packetbeat supports many protocols such as dns, memcache, icmp, http, and so on. We can uncomment the protocol and add additional ports in case we are not using the default ports. The following screenshot shows the protocol section of the **Packetbeat** configuration file:

```
#============================ Transaction protocols ============================

packetbeat.protocols:
- type: icmp
  # Enable ICMPv4 and ICMPv6 monitoring. Default: false
  enabled: true

- type: amqp
  # Configure the ports where to listen for AMQP traffic. You can disable
  # the AMQP protocol by commenting out the list of ports.
  ports: [5672]

- type: cassandra
  #Cassandra port for traffic monitoring.
  ports: [9042]

- type: dhcpv4
  # Configure the DHCP for IPv4 ports.
  ports: [67, 68]

- type: dns
  # Configure the ports where to listen for DNS traffic. You can disable
  # the DNS protocol by commenting out the list of ports.
  ports: [53]

- type: http
  # Configure the ports where to listen for HTTP traffic. You can disable
  # the HTTP protocol by commenting out the list of ports.
  ports: [80, 8080, 8000, 5000, 8002]

- type: memcache
  # Configure the ports where to listen for memcache traffic. You can disable
  # the Memcache protocol by commenting out the list of ports.
  ports: [11211]

- type: mysql
  # Configure the ports where to listen for MySQL traffic. You can disable
```

Figure 5.5: Different protocols of Packetbeat.

The preceding screenshot shows the protocols along with the default ports for the protocol. We can disable the protocol by commenting on them or enable them by uncommenting. After configuring these things, we can restart the Packetbeat service by executing this command:

```
sudo service packetbeat restart
```

This command will restart the Packetbeat service, and it will start fetching the server metrics and send them to the Elasticsearch cluster. Now, we can list all the indices of Elasticsearch to check whether Packetbeat index is created by executing the following command:

```
curl -XGET "http://localhost:9200/_cat/indices?v"
```

The preceding command will list all the indices, and we can see the packetbeat-7.6.1 index there. We can overwrite the index name by providing the index name in the Packetbeat configuration. Now, we can see the index documents by executing the following command:

```
curl -XGET "http://localhost:9200/packetbeat-7.6.1/_search?
```

This command will open the index, and we can see all the documents. The document format is as follows:

```
{
        "_index" : "packetbeat-7.6.1",
        "_type" : "_doc",
        "_id" : "ud3oLHEBGmw9CiLIN4K_",
        "_score" : 1.0,
        "_source" : {
          "@timestamp" : "2020-03-30T19:25:42.878Z",
          "type" : "http",
          "status" : "OK",
          "query" : "GET /",
          "http" : {
            "request" : {
              "method" : "get",
              "bytes" : 87,
              "headers" : {
                "content-length" : 0
              }
            },
```

```
      "response" : {
        "status_phrase" : "no content",
        "status_code" : 204,
        "bytes" : 148,
        "headers" : {
          "content-length" : 0
        }
      },
      "version" : "1.1"
    },
    "event" : {
      "category" : "network_traffic",
      "dataset" : "http",
      "duration" : 308513000,
      "start" : "2020-03-30T19:25:42.878Z",
      "end" : "2020-03-30T19:25:43.187Z",
      "kind" : "event"
    },
    "method" : "get",
    "destination" : {
      "domain" : "connectivity-check.ubuntu.com",
      "bytes" : 148,
      "ip" : "35.222.85.5",
      "port" : 80
    },
    "agent" : {
      "type" : "packetbeat",
      "ephemeral_id" : "bf49c0d8-abed-4622-a631-53b1857da98d",
      "hostname" : "KELLGGNLPTP0305",
      "id" : "0fc28811-d321-4deb-85c4-770e26057127",
      "version" : "7.6.1"
    },
    "client" : {
```

```
      "ip" : "192.168.43.127",
      "port" : 45266,
      "bytes" : 87
    },
    "server" : {
      "ip" : "35.222.85.5",
      "port" : 80,
      "domain" : "connectivity-check.ubuntu.com",
      "bytes" : 148
    },
    "ecs" : {
      "version" : "1.4.0"
    },
    "host" : {
      "name" : "KELLGGNLPTP0305",
      "os" : {
        "version" : "19.04 (Disco Dingo)",
        "family" : "debian",
        "name" : "Ubuntu",
        "kernel" : "5.0.0-38-generic",
        "codename" : "disco",
        "platform" : "ubuntu"
      },
      "id" : "3981136c89ec40e496c3b850831321fe",
      "containerized" : false,
      "hostname" : "KELLGGNLPTP0305",
      "architecture" : "x86_64"
    },
    "source" : {
      "ip" : "192.168.43.127",
      "port" : 45266,
      "bytes" : 87
    },
```

```
"network" : {
  "type" : "ipv4",
  "transport" : "tcp",
  "protocol" : "http",
  "direction" : "outbound",
  "community_id" : "1:knLKYfzzpD83uaa/cbmtYw8Ui50=",
  "bytes" : 235
},
"url" : {
  "path" : "/",
  "full" : "http://connectivity-check.ubuntu.com/",
  "scheme" : "http",
  "domain" : "connectivity-check.ubuntu.com"
  }
 }
}
```

This way, we can configure Packetbeat to read the network packet data and index that in Elasticsearch.

Pulling CSV data using logstash

Till now, we discussed how to import data using Beats, and we saw how to fetch Apache logs, system metrics data, and network packet data, etc. Now, let's see how we can pull CSV data using Logstash. Logstash can be used to fetch data from different sources, such as RDBMS, NoSQL, Kafka, CSV, files, Elasticsearch, logs, and other sources. Logstash is helpful to transform ingested data before sending it to the output. It has three sections: the input section to ingest data from different sources, filter plugin to transform the data before sending it to the output, and the output section to send the data to different destinations. We have already introduced Logstash in *Chapter 3, Working with Elastic Stack*, so you can refer to that chapter for more details. Now, let's understand how we can import data using a CSV file and push it to Elasticsearch, using which we can apply data analysis and visualization. We will use the CSV data with the following format:

```
sno, name, age, gender

1,   lisa, 32,  female

2,   sam,  29,  male

3,   tony, 45,  male

4,   sonia,32,female
```

These records are from a file name `names.csv`, using which we will push these records into Elasticsearch. I have kept the CSV file inside the `Download` directory / `home/user/Downloads/`, but we can put the file anywhere. Just keep in mind that the file must be accessible through Logstash.

Now, we need to create a Logstash configuration file to read this CSV data from the `names.csv` file. So, let's create a `pull_names.conf` `Logstash` configuration file and add the following code snippet:

```
input {
    file {
        path => "/home/user/Downloads/names.csv"
start_position => beginning
    }
}
filter {
  csv {
autodetect_column_names => true
  }
}
output {
stdout
    {
        codec =>rubydebug
    }
elasticsearch {
        action => "index"
        hosts => ["127.0.0.1:9200"]
        index => "names"
        user => elastic
        password =>your_password
    }
}
```

The preceding code snippet shows the Logstash configuration code, where we have three sections: input, filter, and output. In the input section, we are using the file plugin to read the file data. Here, we are providing the file path for the CSV file and the `start_position` is set as the beginning so that Logstash can start from the beginning of the file every time the configuration is executed to pull the CSV data.

The second section is the filter, where we are using the CSV plugin. Here, we are setting `autodetect_column_names` to true so that Logstash can automatically detect the column names from the CSV file itself. We can also provide the field names manually, as shown here:

```
filter {
    csv {
        columns => [
            "id",
            "Name",
            "Age",
            "Gender"
        ]
        separator => ","
        }
}
```

In the preceding code, we provided the field names manually. This way, we can change the label name, but Logstash will use the name given in the CSV file in auto-detect.

The third section is the output section, where we are using the `stdout` plugin to send data to the standard output. The codec rubydebug is there to format the standard output. We are also using the Elasticsearch plugin to send the CSV data to Elasticsearch. In the Elasticsearch plugin, we are providing the action, hosts, index name, username, and password of Elasticsearch.

This way, we can create the Logstash configuration file to fetch the CSV data and send it to Elasticsearch and display the records on the terminal.

Now, we need to execute the Logstash configuration file from the Logstash home using the following command:

bin/logstash -f /etc/logstash/conf.d/pull_names.conf

The preceding command will pull the CSV file data and send it to the standard output as well as Elasticsearch. After executing this command, the first thing we can see is the following output on the terminal:

```
{
        "name" => " lisa",
    "@version" => "1",
```

```
    "@timestamp" => 2020-04-02T12:08:33.436Z,
       "gender" => " female",
           "id" => "1",
         "host" => "KELLGGNLPTP0305",
      "message" => "1, lisa,32, female",
         "path" => "/home/user/Downloads/names.csv",
          "age" => "32"
}
```

The preceding JSON is displayed on the terminal as we are using the `stdout` plugin.

Now, we can list all the indices of Elasticsearch to check whether the names index is created through Logstash by executing the following command:

```
curl -XGET "http://localhost:9200/_cat/indices?v"
```

The preceding command will list all the indices, and we can see the names index there. Now, we can see the index documents by executing the following command:

```
curl -XGET "http://localhost:9200/names/_search?
```

The preceding command will open the index, and we can see all the documents. The document format is as follows:

```
{
        "_index" : "names",
        "_type" : "_doc",
        "_id" : "vqXLOnEBGEvdm4dfC8T7",
        "_score" : 1.0,
        "_source" : {
          "Name" : " sonia",
          "@version" : "1",
          "@timestamp" : "2020-04-02T12:08:33.443Z",
          "Gender" : " female",
          "id" : "4",
          "host" : "KELLGGNLPTP0305",
          "message" : "4, sonia,32, female",
          "path" : "/home/user/Downloads/names.csv",
          "Age" : "32"
        }
}
```

The preceding JSON record shows the Elasticsearch document of the "names" index, which is created through Logstash using the `names.csv` file. This way, we can fetch any file data using Logstash, and we can also fetch records from any RDBSM or NoSQL database, or any other source.

Conclusion

In this chapter, we looked at why data is so important for a business use case. Then, we explored and understood data ingest, data shipping, data storage, and data visualization. We also covered different ways to import the data into Elasticsearch, where we looked at practical examples of some Beats such as Filebeat, Metricbeat, and Packetbeat. Additionally, we learned how to configure Logstash to push data CSV into Elasticsearch.

The next chapter will teach you how to create the index along with mapping. We will then move on to index management, performing index level operations, managing index template, different index APIs, and index life-cycle management.

Questions

1. Explain the importance of data for the business.
2. What is data shipping?
3. What is data ingestion?
4. Import web server logs using Filebeat.
5. Import the server metrics using Metricbeat.
6. Fetch data from a CSV file using Logstash.

CHAPTER 6
Managing Your Index

Introduction

In the last chapter, we covered what data ingest, data shipping, data storage, and data visualization are. Then, we looked at different ways to import data into Elasticsearch, where we saw practical examples of some Beats like Filebeat, Metricbeat, and Packetbeat. We also understood how to push data using Logstash. Now, we will cover index management in this chapter, and we will start with index creation in Elasticsearch and how to create the mapping. After that, we will learn how to manage the Elasticsearch index and how to perform index-level operations. Then, we will look at how to manage the index template. We will also discuss different index level APIs to perform different operations on the index. And at last, we will cover the index lifecycle management.

Structure

In this chapter, we will cover the following topics:

- Creating index along with mapping
- Performing index level operations
- Index management
- Index APIs

- Managing index template
- Index lifecycle management

Objectives

After studying this unit, you should be able to:
- Create the index
- Perform different operations on Elasticsearch indices
- Configure the index lifecycle

Creating index along with mapping

In Elasticsearch, we can create the index to keep similar types of records; it is similar to a table in the relational database. We can create multiple indices in Elasticsearch, and each index can have multiple documents. We can create the index using Elasticsearch "create index API" through a PUT request. The Elasticsearch index can be created using different ways, like by creating a blank index without using any document or by indexing the document that automatically creates the index. We can also create index through different sources like by pushing data from different Beats or Logstash. In the previous chapter, we saw that we can automatically create the Elasticsearch index using Beats and Logstash.

Creating an index without any document

Now, let's see how we can create the Elasticsearch index without adding any document by executing the following command:

```
curl -XPUT "http://localhost:9200/testindex"
```

Using this command, we can create the `testindex`, and it will return the following output:

```
{
  "acknowledged" : true,
  "shards_acknowledged" : true,
  "index" : "testindex"
}
```

The preceding response shows the JSON with index name, acknowledged as true and `shard_acknowledged` as true. So, if we are getting true for the acknowledged, the index is created successfully. We can get the details of the index by executing the following command:

```
curl -XGET "http://localhost:9200/testindex"
```

After executing the preceding command, we get the following response:

```
{
  "testindex" : {
    "aliases" : { },
    "mappings" : { },
    "settings" : {
      "index" : {
        "number_of_shards" : "1",
        "blocks" : {
          "read_only_allow_delete" : "true"
        },
        "provided_name" : "testindex",
        "creation_date" : "1586008632727",
        "number_of_replicas" : "1",
        "uuid" : "10Ml40m9QEaM4uYaDL-dXw",
        "version" : {
          "created" : "7060199"
        }
      }
    }
  }
}
```

This response shows details like index name, its mapping, which is blank because we have not provided the mapping details during index creation, the number of shards, creation date, UUID, version, and the number of replicas, etc.

If we try to create an index that is already created, Elasticsearch will throw a **400** error. Here's the response that Elasticsearch will return if we try to create the same index again using the preceding create index command:

```
{
  "error" : {
    "root_cause" : [
      {
```

```
        "type" : "resource_already_exists_exception",
      "reason" : "index [testindex/10Ml40m9QEaM4uYaDL-dXw] already exists",
         "index_uuid" : "10Ml40m9QEaM4uYaDL-dXw",
         "index" : "testindex"
      }
    ],
    "type" : "resource_already_exists_exception",
    "reason" : "index [testindex/10Ml40m9QEaM4uYaDL-dXw] already exists",
    "index_uuid" : "10Ml40m9QEaM4uYaDL-dXw",
    "index" : "testindex"
  },
  "status" : 400
}
```

In this response, we can see the error root cause in the form of a JSON document. It shows the type as `resource_already_exists_exception` and the reason as `index [testindex/tELbHSktSPipCPYfMW_Qug] already exist"`. This way, whenever we try to create an already created index, Elasticsearch will throw a `400` error with the above-mentioned error message.

Creating index along with the documents

Elasticsearch automatically creates the index for us when we post the first document without creating the index first. Now, let's see how we can create the index with initial documents, unlike the above example where we have just created the index without adding any document. The following example shows the command using to create the index with a document:

```
curl -XPOST "http://localhost:9200/testindex/_doc/1" -H 'Content-Type:
application/json' -d'{ "name": "Anurag", "gender":"male", "city":"New
Delhi"}'
```

The following command shows the JSON representation of the above-mentioned CURL query that we can execute from Kibana:

```
POST testindex/_doc/1
{
  "name": "Anurag",
  "gender":"male",
  "city":"New Delhi"
}
```

The preceding command shows the index creation with the document with ID as 1. This way, we can create the index by inserting the document. We can get the document by executing the following command:

```
curl -XGET "http://localhost:9200/testindex/_doc/1/"
```

In this command, we are trying to fetch the document with the ID as 1. After executing the preceding command, we get the following response:

```
{
  "_index" : "testindex",
  "_type" : "_doc",
  "_id" : "1",
  "_version" : 2,
  "_seq_no" : 2,
  "_primary_term" : 1,
  "found" : true,
  "_source" : {
    "name" : "Anurag",
    "gender" : "male",
    "city" : "New Delhi"
  }
}
```

There is an issue when we directly index the document without explicitly creating the mapping. This is because Elasticsearch guesses the data type of the document fields we are trying to index, but that guess is not always correct. It is very much required to map the fields with the exact type of data each field contains.

Get mapping of the index

Now, let's see how we can get the mapping details of an index as it is required to know the data type of different fields. Using the following command, we can get the mapping details of the index:

```
curl -XGET "http://localhost:9200/testindex/_mapping"
```

We get the following output from this command:

```
{
  "testindex" : {
    "mappings" : {
      "properties" : {
```

```
      "city" : {
        "type" : "text",
        "fields" : {
          "keyword" : {
            "type" : "keyword",
            "ignore_above" : 256
          }
        }
      },
      "gender" : {
        "type" : "text",
        "fields" : {
          "keyword" : {
            "type" : "keyword",
            "ignore_above" : 256
          }
        }
      },
      "name" : {
        "type" : "text",
        "fields" : {
          "keyword" : {
            "type" : "keyword",
            "ignore_above" : 256
          }
        }
      }
    }
  }
}
```

The preceding JSON shows the mapping of the testindex, where we can see the field names along with the data type and whether the field is a keyword type.

Create a mapping of the index

Now, let's see how we can create the mapping of an index as it is required to create it explicitly if we don't want Elasticsearch to guess it for us. Using the following command, we can create the mapping for an index:

```
PUT newindex
```

We first need to create the new index using the preceding command, and then we can set the mapping of different fields of the index with the following one:

```
PUT newindex/_mappings
{
  "properties": {
      "firstname": {
        "type": "keyword"
      },
      "lastname": {
        "type": "keyword"
      },
      "account_number": {
        "type": "integer"
      },
      "balance": {
        "type": "integer"
      },
      "age": {
        "type": "integer"
      },
      "gender": {
        "type": "keyword"
      }
   }
}
```

Using this command, we can create the mapping in the index, but we have to keep in mind that there is no document in indexed before the mapping creation. In the newindex index, we have the following fields:

- firstname
- lastname

- account_number
- balance
- age
- gender

Now based on the data type of these fields, we have created the mapping where the firstname, lastname, and gender fields are string. So, we have mapped them with the keyword so that they can be searched as a keyword. The account_number, balance, and age fields are integer, so we have mapped them as an integer.

After creating the mapping of the index, we can see the index mapping using the given command:

```
curl -XGET "http://localhost:9200/newindex/_mapping"
```

This command will output the following JSON:

```
{
  "newindex" : {
    "mappings" : {
      "properties" : {
        "account_number" : {
          "type" : "integer"
        },
        "age" : {
          "type" : "integer"
        },
        "balance" : {
          "type" : "integer"
        },
        "firstname" : {
          "type" : "keyword"
        },
        "gender" : {
          "type" : "keyword"
        },
        "lastname" : {
          "type" : "keyword"
        }
```

```
        }
      }
    }
  }
}
```

We can see the mapping of the index as it shows the data type of each field of the index. This way, we can create the mapping on any Elasticsearch index.

Index management

Index management is available under Kibana UI, and we can view the index settings, mappings, statistics, and such using it. We can access index management by clicking on the **Management** link from the left menu, which will open the **Management** page. On the **Management** page, click on the **Index Management** option to open the following page:

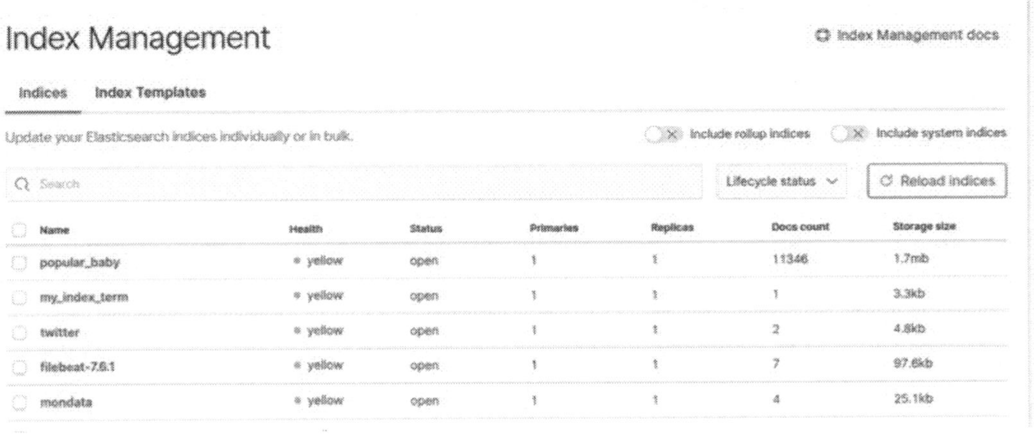

Figure 6.1: Index management

This screenshot shows the index management page of Kibana, where we can see the list of indices with the health, status, count of primaries, replicas, docs count, storage size, etc. We can perform different operations on the indices, like show to index settings, mapping, stats, or edit the index setting, close index, flush index, delete index.

Using index management, we can perform different index-level operations like the refreshing, force merging segments, freezing indices, clearing the cache, flushing, and several other options. We can perform bulk operations on multiple indices. Kibana index management option shows badge on the listing page to show whether the index is frozen, a rollup index, or a follower index. The badge can also be used for filtering the list.

Performing index-level operations

We can perform several index-level operations using the Manage index option on the Index Management page. Refer to the following screenshot:

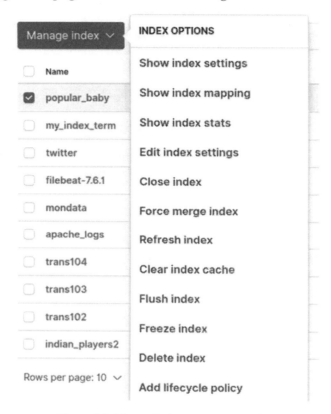

Figure 6.2: Manage index pop-up screenshot.

The preceding screenshot shows the dropdown screen with different options of the **Manage index** dropdown. We can perform different index-level operations on a single index or in bulk using the **Manage index** option on the **Kibana Management** page. These index-level operations include the following:

Close index

Using the close index option, we can block the index so that it is unavailable for any read or write operation. We can perform this operation on single or multiple indices. A closed index only consumes disk space and no other resources. If we want to bring it back, we can reopen it by recovering the index through a normal recovery process.

Delete index

Using the delete index option, we can delete one or many indices. It also deletes all of the documents of the indices that we are going to delete. We also have REST APIs to perform these operations, and we will cover them in the next section.

Freeze index

Using the freeze option, we can make an index read-only. By freezing an index, we can reduce its memory footprint as it moves its shards to the disk. We can perform the search operation on the frozen index, but it will take a bit longer, as Elasticsearch has to retrieve the results from the disk. The write operations are blocked on frozen indices.

Refresh index

Using the refresh index option, we can explicitly refresh one or more indices. By default, Elasticsearch refreshes the indices every second, but we can explicitly refresh anytime using this option. The automatic refresh will work only if the Elasticsearch index has received one or more search requests in the last 30 seconds. This interval is defined in the `index.refresh_interval` setting, and we can change it if required. The Elasticsearch refresh operation is very much resource-intensive, so it is not advisable to explicitly refresh the indices. Instead, we should wait for the periodic refresh of Elasticsearch.

Force merge index

The force merge index operation merges smaller shard files that reduce the number of segments in the shard. This operation also clears deleted documents, and we can force merge a read-only index with this option.

Clear index cache

Using this operation, we can clear all caches that are there for an index.

Flush index

Using the flush index option, we can synchronize the filesystem cache to the disk. Using this, we can free the memory and ensure that any data in the transactional log is pushed to the Lucene index and is permanently stored.

Add lifecycle policy

Using this option, we can configure the policy for index lifecycle management. Using the policy, we can define the actions to be performed on an index as it ages, and these policies are more suitable for time series data, for example, Beats data. We can apply the index rollover to a new index by applying the condition if the existing index reaches a certain size or given age duration. This ensures a smaller size of the index, in which we can easily perform the search, etc.

Index APIs

Elasticsearch provides REST-based APIs, using which we can perform different operations on indices. In the previous section, we discussed some of the index-level operations that we can perform using the Index Management option of Kibana management. We can perform all these operations using index APIs as well, and the APIs also provide more options than the Management UI. We can manage individual indices, their mappings, index template, aliases, and index settings, etc using index APIs. In this chapter, we won't cover all the index APIs but will discuss the important ones. Let's start with the index management APIs.

Index management

Under this category, we will cover the APIs using which we can manage the index. These APIs include the create index, delete index, get index, close index, open index, clone index, and freeze index.

Creating an index

We can create a new index using the create index API. We can also do the following with an index creation:

- Change the index settings
- Set the mapping of the index
- Create index aliases

We can create an index using the following command:

```
PUT /<index_name>
```

Using the preceding command, we can create the index. The index name has the following criteria that we must follow:

- The index name must be in lowercase.
- It cannot include the characters # , ,, \, /, *, ?, ", <, >, |, ` ` (space character)

- Colon (:) was supported in index name before 7.0 version, but it is deprecated from version 7.0 onward.
- The index name cannot start with the _, -, + signs.
- It must not be longer than 255 bytes.

The create index API supports query parameters like `include_type_name, wait_for_active_shards, timeout, master_timeout`, etc. Using these parameters, we can set these options using the index creation. We can also put the request body with this API to perform additional operations. It supports the aliases, mappings, and settings options in the request body, using which we can create aliases, create index mapping, or change the settings of the index.

Delete index

We can delete any index using the following endpoint:

```
DELETE /<index_name>
```

We can delete an index by hitting the `DELETE` request with the name of the index using the preceding expression. We can delete all indices using the `_all` or `*` expression in the query.

The delete index API supports different query expressions like `allow_no_indices, expand_wildcard, ignore_unavailable, timeout, master_timeout`. We can tweak the delete operation using these parameters.

Get index

Using the get index API, we can return the information of one or more indices. The expression for the get index API is as follows:

```
GET /<index_name>
```

In the preceding expression, we have the `GET` request with the index name, using which we can fetch the index information.

In the path parameter, we can use `_all` to retrieve all the indices instead of any specific index. We can also provide a comma-separated list of indices to get details of only those indices. There are some query parameters that we can use with the get index API, like `allow_no_indices, expand_wildcards, flat_settings, include_defaults, include_type_name, ignore_unavailable, local, master_timeout`, etc. Using these parameters, we can tweak the API behavior.

Close index

We can close the open indices using a close index API. Using the following expression, we can close the index:

```
POST /<index_name>/_close
```

In the preceding expression, we can make a `POST` request with the index name and add the `_close` parameter to close the index. Unlike an open index, the closed index does not support any read or write operations as it is blocked for these operations. We cannot index documents or search documents from a closed index. We can close all indices by providing `_all` as a path parameter instead of the index name.

The close index API also supports different query parameters, like `allow_no_indices`, `expand_wildcards`, `ignore_unavailable`, `wait_for_active_shards`, `timeout`, `master_timeout`, etc. Using this option, we can tweak the close operation. For example, if we want to close the index, we can execute the following command:

```
POST testindex/_close
```

Using the above-mentioned command, we can close `testindex`, and it will provide the following output:

```
{
    "acknowledged" : true,
    "shards_acknowledged" : true,
    "indices" : {
        "testindex" : {
            "closed" : true
        }
    }
}
```

Now if we want to perform any operation on the index like the search then we need to first open it and for that we can use the open index API.

Open index

We can open the closed index using the open index API. A closed index is closed for read and write operations and has a lower memory footprint. We can open a closed index using the following expression:

```
POST /<index_name>/_open
```

Using this expression, we can open a closed index through a post request by typing the index name and _open as a parameter. We can open all closed indices by providing `_all` as a path parameter instead of the index name.

The open index API also supports different query parameters, like `allow_no_indices`, `expand_wildcards`, `ignore_unavailable`, `wait_for_active_shards`, `timeout`, `master_timeout`, etc. Using this option, we can tweak the open operation. For example, if we want to open the closed `testindex` index, we must execute the following command:

```
POST /testindex/_open
```

We will get the following response:

```
{
    "acknowledged" : true,
    "shards_acknowledged" : true
}
```

This way, we can open the closed indices using the open index API.

Index Exist API

Using the index exist API, we can know whether the index is available in the Elasticsearch cluster. We can execute the following command to know whether the index exists in the Elasticsearch cluster:

```
HEAD /<index_name>
```

This command will return the status code with a message and returns the response codes **200** or **404**. The response code **200** is returned when the indices or the aliases exist in the cluster. The response code **404** is returned when the specified indices or aliases are not available. For example, if we want to know whether an index is present in the Elasticsearch cluster, we can execute the following command:

```
HEAD newindex
```

We will receive the following response:

```
200 - OK
```

So, the response we are getting here is **200**, which means the index is available in the Elasticsearch cluster. In the path parameter, we can mention the name of indices in a comma-separated way if we want to know the status of multiple indices. The index exists API also supports different query parameters, like `allow_no_indices`, `expand_wildcards`, `ignore_unavailable`, `flat_settings`, `include_defaults`, `local`, etc. Using these options, we can tweak the operation of the index exists API.

Shrink index

We can shrink an existing index using the shrink index API. It reduces the count of primary shards, so we can execute the following expression to shrink any index:

```
POST /<existing_index>/_shrink/<new_index>
```

In the above expression, we need to make a POST request by mentioning the index name we want to shrink. After that, we must provide the `_shrink` ion with the first URI segment, and then we must provide the name of the new shrunk index.

We must check a few conditions before shrinking any index:

- The index has to be read-only.
- The copy of each shard must be on the same node.
- The health of the cluster has to be green.

Once these conditions are met, we can shrink the index. The index shrink API also supports different query parameters, like `wait_for_active_shards,` `timeout`, and `master_timeout`. Using these options, we can tweak the shrink API operation. This API also supports request body for aliases and settings option, using which we can set the index aliases or change the index settings as well.

Freeze index

Using the freeze index API, we can freeze the index as it removes the index overhead on the cluster. Frozen indices are read-only, and they are blocked for any write operations. They have almost no memory footprint as only the frozen index metadata is maintained in the memory. The following expression can be used to freeze an index:

```
POST /<index_name>/_freeze
```

In the preceding expression, using a `POST` request, we can freeze the index just by providing the index name and passing `_freeze` as an URL parameter.

Unfreeze index

We can unfreeze a frozen index using the unfreeze index API. During the unfreezing process, the index becomes writeable again through a normal recovery process. Wr must execute the following command to unfreeze a frozen index:

```
POST /<index_name>/_unfreeze
```

We can pass the frozen index name by executing the above command, and the index would be available for write operations after the command execution.

Split index

We can split an index to a new index by increasing the primary shards. We must execute the following expression to split an index:

```
POST /<index_name>/_split/<new_index>
```

In the preceding expression, we have a POST request, where we are providing the existing index name. After that, we are using the _split keyword, and, finally, we must provide the new index name that we want to create by splitting the old index.

We can use the following expression to split the newindex index:

```
POST /newindex/_split/split-newindex
{
  "settings": {
    "index.number_of_shards": 2
  }
}
```

In the preceding expression, we are splitting the newindex to the split-newindex index. After executing the above-mentioned command, we will get the following response:

```
{
  "acknowledged" : true,
  "shards_acknowledged" : true,
  "index" : "split-newindex"
}
```

This way, we can split the index by increasing the primary shards. The split index API also supports different query parameters, like wait_for_active_shards, timeout, and master_timeout. Using these options, we can tweak the split API operation. This API also supports request body for aliases and settings option, which can be used to set the index aliases or change the index settings as well.

Clone index

We can clone an index using the clone index API. The structure of clone index API is as follows:

```
POST /<index_name>/_clone/<target_index_name>
```

In the preceding example, we can clone index_name to the target_index_name using the _clone keyword of the clone index API.

We have to meet the following conditions before creating the clone of an index:

- The index should be marked as read-only.
- The cluster health status should be green.

The clone index API works as mentioned here:

- Firstly, it creates the target index using the same source index definition.
- Next, it hard-links segments of the source index to the target index, and all segments are copied from source index to the target index if hard-linking is not allowed.
- In the final step, it recovers the target index in the same way it does for a closed index by reopening it.

For example, if we want to clone `newindex`, we can follow these steps:

1. The first step is to block the write operation on the index using the following expression:

```
PUT /testindex/_settings
{
  "settings": {
    "index.blocks.write": true
  }
}
```

2. Now, we can create the clone index using the given expression:

```
POST /testindex/_clone/newtestindex
```

3. After executing the preceding command, we get the following response:

```
{
  "acknowledged" : true,
  "shards_acknowledged" : true,
  "index" : "newtestindex"
}
```

This way, we can clone an index using the source index. The clone index API also supports different query parameters, like `wait_for_active_shards`, `timeout`, and `master_timeout`. Using these options, we can tweak the clone API operation. This API also supports request body for aliases and settings option, which can be used to set the index aliases or change the index settings.

Rollover index

Using the rollover index API, we can apply conditions using which an index alias can be assigned to a new index. These conditions can be based on the age of index, the maximum number of documents, or the max size of the index. For example, we can use the following expression to apply the index rollover using the alias:

```
POST /<alias_name>/_rollover/<index_name>
{
    "conditions": {
        "max_age": "15d",
        "max_docs": 2000,
        "max_size": "15gb"
    }
}
```

Using this expression, we can set the index rollover. Here, we have multiple conditions, like the max age is 15 days, the max number of documents is 2000, and the max index size is 15GB. If any of the conditions are met, the alias will be assigned to a new index. This will ensure that the index size does not exceed the given limit, so we can retire an index if it becomes too large or too old.

This API will not work as a scheduler. So this API will check the condition and assign the alias to a new index accordingly. After executing the API, Elasticsearch will not monitor the conditions. If we want to automate this process, we have to use the Index Lifecycle Management (ILM) policies.

The rollover index API works as follows:

- In the first step, it creates a new index based on the given conditions.
- It then assigns the alias with the new index and sets the `is_write_index` flag to `true` for the new index.
- Next, it removes the assignment of alias with the original index and sets the `is_write_index` flag to `false` for the original index.

The index rollover API also supports different query parameters, like `dry_run`, `include_type_name`, `wait_for_active_shards`, `timeout`, and `master_timeout`. Using these options, we can tweak the index rollover API operation. This API also supports request body for aliases, conditions, mappings, and settings option, using which we can set the index aliases or change the index settings.

For example, if we want to configure the rollover on an index using the index rollover API, we must do the following:

1. Create an index with the alias. Here, we have to provide the index name by appending it with a 6-digit number with a hyphen. The number has to be zero-padded and should start at 1. for example, index-`000001`. The index rollover API will increment this number to create further indices, like index-`000001` will be incremented to index-`000002`. The following expression shows the creation of the index with alias:

```
PUT /new_roll_index-000001
```

```
{
  "aliases": {
    "roll_alias": {
      "logs": { "is_write_index": true }
    }
  }
}
```

2. After executing this expression, we can create the index with the alias. We will now execute the index rollover API for applying the conditions. Refer to the following expression:

```
POST /roll_alias/_rollover
{
  "conditions": {
    "max_age":   "7d",
    "max_docs":  1000,
    "max_size": "5gb"
  }
}
```

In the preceding expression, we are adding three conditions, using which the index rollover API will create other indices and map the alias to the new index. After executing the preceding command, we will get the following response:

```
{
  "acknowledged" : false,
  "shards_acknowledged" : false,
  "old_index" : "new_roll_index-000001",
  "new_index" : "new_roll_index-000002",
  "rolled_over" : false,
  "dry_run" : false,
  "conditions" : {
    "[max_docs: 1000]" : false,
    "[max_size: 5gb]" : false,
    "[max_age: 7d]" : false
  }
}
```

The preceding response show acknowledged as false because the condition was not met with an existing index. This way, we can configure the rollover process to limit the index size, which will improve performance.

Index settings

In this section, we will cover the APIs to change the index settings. These APIs include update index settings, get index settings, and analyze.

Update index settings

We can change the index settings in real-time using the update index settings API, including the number of replicas, refresh interval, etc. For example, if we want to change the number of replicas to 2, we can execute the following expression:

```
PUT /newindex/_settings
{
    "index" : {
        "number_of_replicas" : 2
    }
}
```

We will get the following response:

```
{
  "acknowledged" : true
}
```

The update index settings API also supports different query parameters, like `allow_no_indices`, `expand_wildcards`, `flat_settings`, `ignore_unavailable`, `preserve_existing`, `timeout`, and `master_timeout`. Using these options, we can tweak the update index settings API operation. This API supports the request body for settings option, using which we can change the index settings. We can reset a setting to default using the null value against that setting; for example, we can execute the following command to reset `refresh_interval` to its default value:

```
PUT /newindex/_settings
{
    "index" : {
        "refresh_interval" : null
    }
}
```

This way, we can use the update index settings API for changing the index settings.

Get index settings

The get index settings API returns the index settings. We can see the index settings using the following expression:

```
GET /<index_name>/_settings
```

The preceding expression can be used to see the settings of any index. For example, we can execute the following command if we want to see the settings of `newindex`:

```
GET /newindex/_settings
```

After executing the above-mentioned command, we will get the following response:

```
{
  "newindex" : {
    "settings" : {
      "index" : {
        "number_of_shards" : "1",
        "blocks" : {
          "read_only_allow_delete" : "true"
        },
        "provided_name" : "newindex",
        "creation_date" : "1586021401751",
        "number_of_replicas" : "2",
        "uuid" : "68hXo41gR9Wzb5_U1AdXWQ",
        "version" : {
          "created" : "7060199",
          "upgraded" : "7060299"
        }
      }
    }
  }
}
```

It provides details like the number of shards, whether read-only is allowed, whether the delete flag is true or false, the provided name, creation date, the number of replicas, UUID, and version details. This way, we can get the index setting using the get index settings API. This API also supports different query parameters, like `allow_no_indices, expand_wildcards, flat_settings, include_defaults, ignore_unavailable, local`, and `master_timeout`. Using these options, we can tweak the get index settings API operation.

Manage index templates

Index templates are used to define a template that can be automatically applied when a new index is created. A template contains the settings and mappings of the index, along with a simple pattern template that controls whether the template should be applied to a new index. There are different index template APIs to manage the index template.

Creating an index template

Using the put index template API, we can create or update an index template. We can create an index template using the following expression:

```
PUT _template/test_template
{
  "index_patterns": ["an*", "test*"],
  "settings": {
    "number_of_shards": 1
  },
  "mappings": {
    "_source": {
      "enabled": false
    },
    "properties": {
      "host_name": {
        "type": "keyword"
      },
      "created_at": {
        "type": "date",
        "format": "EEE MMM dd HH:mm:ss Z yyyy"
      }
    }
  }
}
```

Using this expression, we can create the `test_template` with the setting for the number of shards as 1 and mapping for the `host_name` property as keyword type and the `created_at` field as a date type. We have also provided an* and test* for the `index_patterns` field so that the template can be applied on any index that starts with an or test. After executing the preceding expression, we will get the following response:

```
{
  "acknowledged" : true
}
```

The index template only works during index creation, so any change in the index template will not affect an index created earlier. We can also use C-style /* */ block comments in the index template.

The put index template API also supports different query parameters, like create, order, and `master_timeout`. Using these options, we can tweak the put index template API operation. This API supports the request body for `index_patters`, aliases, and mappings option, using which we can define aliases and mappings and put the patterns for the matching indices.

Get index template

Using the get index template API, we can get the information about one or more index template. To get the index template details, we can execute the following command:

```
GET _template/test_template
```

After executing this command, we will get the following response:

```
{
  "test_template" : {
    "order" : 0,
    "index_patterns" : [
      "an*",
      "test*"
    ],
    "settings" : {
      "index" : {
        "number_of_shards" : "1"
      }
    },
```

```
  "mappings" : {
    "_source" : {
      "enabled" : false
    },
    "properties" : {
      "created_at" : {
        "format" : "EEE MMM dd HH:mm:ss Z yyyy",
        "type" : "date"
      },
      "host_name" : {
        "type" : "keyword"
      }
    }
  },
  "aliases" : { }
 }
}
```

Delete index template

We can delete an index template using the following command:

```
DELETE _template/test_template
```

We can delete the `test_template` index template using the preceding command. We can delete multiple index templates by providing a comma-separated list or wildcard expression.

Index lifecycle management

Using the index lifecycle policy, we can define the rules and when to perform certain actions based on that. For example, when we want to rollover or force merge the index. We discussed that rollover APIs work once, and we can use index lifecycle policy to automate such actions. Although we have APIs to create the index lifecycle policy, it is quite simple to create it using the Kibana UI interface, so let's look at that in this chapter. To create the index lifecycle policy using Kibana, we must do the following:

- After opening the Kibana interface, click on the **Management** link from the left menu and then on the **Index Lifecycle Policy** link from the management screen. This will open the **Create an index lifecycle policy** page.

- Then, provide the name of the policy. Under the hot phase, click on the **Enable rollover** slider to enable it and set the options like maximum index size, maximum documents, and maximum age.

- After that, we can configure the warm phase and cold phase with different options, like if we want to freeze or shrink the index to save memory.

- We can also configure the delete phase to delete the index after certain days of rollover.

- After configuring these settings, we can click on the **Save as new policy** button to create the policy.

Once the policy is created, we can see it on the listing page of index lifecycle policies. From the right side, we can see the **Action** link, using which we can add policy with the index template and view the indices linked to the policy. This way, we can create the index lifecycle policy and attach it with the index template.

Conclusion

In this chapter, we covered everything related to Elasticsearch index management, like how to create an index and how to put index mapping. We also learned how to perform some index-level operations and moved on to index-level REST APIs that are quite helpful when we play around an Elasticsearch index. After that, we discussed the index template and how to manage it, and finally, we walked through index lifecycle management.

The next chapter will cover how to apply search on your data. We will start with URI search and move to body search. After that, we will cover the search and multi-search template and multi-search API. We will also cover the explain API to understand how it will help us, and we will look at the profile API. Stay tuned to learn how to search for data in Elasticsearch.

Questions

1. How can we create an index in Elasticsearch?

2. How can we create index mapping?

3. How can we create an index and add some documents to the index.

4. How can we close, open, and delete an index?

5. How can we get and update the index settings?

6. How can we get and create the index template?

## CHAPTER 7

Applying Search on Your Data

Introduction

In the last chapter, we covered index management, where we explained index creation and how to create the mapping. After that, we looked at how to manage the Elasticsearch index and perform index-level operations. We also learned how to manage the index template, various index-level APIs, and index life-cycle management.

In this chapter, we will cover data search using Elasticsearch. We will start with URI search and move on to performing the body search. We will discuss search and multi-search templates and cover the multi-search API. Then, we will look at the explain API and profile APIs. The purpose of the search is to get relevant information from a data source, and with data size increasing day by day, it is very important to fetch the relevant information from that data. Elasticsearch provides us with different ways to search data, where we can tweak them to get the most relevant information.

Structure

In this chapter, we will cover the following:

- URI search
- Request body search

- Multi-search API and template
- Explain API
- Profile API

Objective

After studying this unit, you should be able to:

- Perform the URI search
- Perform the body search
- Use the Explain API to tune the performance

In Elasticsearch, every field of a document is indexed so that we can apply queries on all of them. We can apply a query on a single index, or it can be performed across multiple indices. We can perform different types of searches, like searching the concrete fields like age, roll number, and contact number, or it can be a full-text search to find matching documents with a search keyword, or it can be a combination of both in a single query. The simplest way is to perform a URI search, so let's start the URI search to understand how we can construct the query to fetch the results.

URI search

In Elasticsearch, we can perform the search by passing the search keywords in the URI. The most basic URI search is an empty search, so let's understand how we can perform an empty search.

Empty search

The empty search is the most basic search where we don't specify any query and can fetch all documents across all indices. Using the following query, we can fetch all documents from all indices:

```
GET /_search
```

The preceding query will output documents from all available indices in the Elasticsearch. If we want to return document from any specific index, we must provide the index name before the _search endpoint. Refer to the following command:

```
GET userdetails/_search
```

This query will return all documents of the userdetails index. Now, if we want to see the documents from multiple indices, we can pass the index names in a comma separated form. In the following example, we will fetch the documents from two indices:

```
GET userdetails,companies/_search
```

We can list all the documents of index `userdetails` and companies using the preceding command. Similarly, we can pass the index names in a comma-separated way to list down the documents.

We can also use the wildcard to fetch all documents with the index names that match the wildcard criteria. Refer to the following example:

```
GET u*,m*/_search
```

Here, we are fetching all documents from indices that start with the characters u and m. This way, we can fetch documents from a single index, multiple indices, or from all indices of the cluster.

Field search

In Elasticsearch URI search, we pass the search term in the URI as a parameter. We can use the term for quick search, where we cannot provide any other search option. For example, we will refer the following `userdetails` index and perform the data search:

```
{
  "_index" : "userdetails",
  "_type" : "_doc",
  "_id" : "2",
  "_version" : 1,
  "_seq_no" : 3,
  "_primary_term" : 1,
  "found" : true,
  "_source" : {
    "name" : "Suresh",
    "gender" : "male",
    "city" : "Singapore",
    "age" : 32
  }
}
```

In the preceding index document, we have the `name,` `gender`, and `city` fields available. Now, if we want to search for a name `Anurag` from this index, we can construct a URI query as follows:

```
GET userdetails/_search?q=name:Anurag
```

Using this command, we can fetch the name `Anurag` by placing this term in the URI against the q parameter. So, we can put the key name and concatenate it with the field value using a colon sign to search a value against a field name. The preceding query will return the following:

```
{
  "took" : 26,
  "timed_out" : false,
  "_shards" : {
    "total" : 1,
    "successful" : 1,
    "skipped" : 0,
    "failed" : 0
  },
  "hits" : {
    "total" : {
      "value" : 1,
      "relation" : "eq"
    },
    "max_score" : 1.2039728,
    "hits" : [
      {
        "_index" : "userdetails",
        "_type" : "_doc",
        "_id" : "3",
        "_score" : 1.2039728,
        "_source" : {
          "name" : "Anurag",
          "gender" : "male",
          "city" : "New Delhi",
          "age" : 37
        }
      }
    ]
  }
}
```

Now, let's understand the result output structure by breaking the structure to understand the meaning of that section. Refer to the following section:

```
"took" : 26,
  "timed_out" : false,
```

Here, took shows the time in milliseconds and tells the time that Elasticsearch took to process the request. The `timed_out` field tells whether the query is timed out. We can also provide the timeout parameter in the query to explicitly timeout after a specific duration. If we receive the `timed_out` value as true, it means Elasticsearch shows the results extracted before the timeout and may not include all the results. Now, move to the next section and refer to the following snippet:

```
"_shards" : {
    "total" : 1,
    "successful" : 1,
    "skipped" : 0,
    "failed" : 0
  }
```

This expression shows that Elasticsearch has searched the results from 1 shard, and it was successful. Also, it has not skipped any shard, and there is no failure. The next section is hits statistics; refer to the following expression:

```
"hits" : {
    "total" : {
      "value" : 1,
      "relation" : "eq"
    },
    "max_score" : 1.2039728
```

The preceding expression shows the hits stats, where `total.value` shows the total matched documents. The `total.relation` shows the type as equal (eq) when `track_total_hits` is set to true. The `max_score` shows the maximum score of the matching documents. The `max_score` in Elasticsearch is generated after `_score` for all matching documents is generated. It would be the maximum `_score` for all matching documents in an Elasticsearch query. The last hits array is the actual result document we get in the response; refer to the following snippet:

```
"hits" : [
    {
      "_index" : "userdetails",
```

```
"_type" : "_doc",
"_id" : "3",
"_score" : 1.2039728,
"_source" : {
  "name" : "Anurag",
  "gender" : "male",
  "city" : "New Delhi",
"age" : 37
  }
}
```

The preceding array shows individual documents where we can see the index name, type, id, and score, etc. Type shows the Elasticsearch document type, id is unique for each Elasticsearch document, and the score is calculated based on the matching algorithm of Elasticsearch. Under the source field, we can get the actual document values, which are name, gender, city, and age. This way, we can interpret the Elasticsearch query result.

We can pass some parameters in the URI search:

- q: The q parameter is used to represent the query string where we can mention the search keyword along with the field name; for example, filedname:keyword. Take a look at the following expression:

```
GET userdetails/_search?q=name:A*
```

This expression shows the q parameter, where we are using the wildcard * so that the name field can be searched against all the names that start with A.

- size: By default, Elasticsearch shows 10 records, so we can change the number of records by providing the size parameter. Refer to the given expression:

```
GET userdetails/_search?q=name:A*&size=3
```

With this expression, we can use the size parameter to limit the size to 3 instead of the default 10.

- from: Using the from parameter, we can set the starting index of the result. By default, Elasticsearch starts with index 0:

```
GET userdetails/_search?q=name:A*&from=2
```

Here, we are using the from parameter to start the results from index 2 instead of the default index, which is 0 in Elasticsearch.

- sort: We can apply the sorting on any field by providing the field name along with the type of sorting; for example, fieldname:asc or fieldname:desc to sort the fieldname in ascending or descending order. Refer to the expression given here:

```
GET userdetails/_search?q=name:A*&sort=age:asc
```

Here, we are sorting the results as per the user age in ascending order. Instead of asc, we can mention desc to sort the results in descending order.

- analyzer: We can also pass the analyzer in the Elasticsearch URI search query. This way, we can explicitly select the analyzer for the query. Refer to this expression:

```
GET userdetails/_search?q=name:A*&analyzer=stop
```

This query shows the analyzer parameter, which is set to the stop analyzer. This way, we can specify the analyzer in the URI search query.

- explain: Using the explain parameter, we can get the details of how the scoring of a document was computed for every hit. Refer to the following expression:

```
GET userdetails/_search?q=name:A*&explain=true
```

Using this command with the explain parameter, we can get the following response:

```
{
  "_shard" : "[userdetails][0]",
  "_node" : "OsuaWgbGQd2KXbWE3ENfEg",
  "_index" : "userdetails",
  "_type" : "_doc",
  "_id" : "4",
  "_score" : 1.0,
  "_source" : {
    "name" : "Amar",
    "gender" : "male",
    "city" : "Mumbai",
    "age" : 30
  },
  "_explanation" : {
    "value" : 1.0,
    "description" : "name:a*",
```

```
            "details" : [ ]
        }
    }
```

The precding response shows additional details like shard and node names, along with the explanation for the scoring.

Request body search

Elasticsearch request body uses query **DSL(domain-specific language)**, which works as an API layer to execute raw Elasticsearch queries. Using request body queries, we can easily construct complex search queries and data aggregation queries using a convenient and clean syntax. We will learn how to construct queries through the request body by using the Kibana DevTools to write and execute the queries.

To understand how we can write a request body query, we will execute the same URI query using the body; refer to the given expression:

```
GET userdetails/_search
{
  "query": {
    "term": {
      "name": {
        "value": "anurag"
      }
    }
  }
}
```

In the preceding query, we are searching the document with name as `anurag` by constructing a query to match the term value with `anurag`. After executing the expression, we will get the following response:

```
{
  "took" : 0,
  "timed_out" : false,
  "_shards" : {
    "total" : 1,
    "successful" : 1,
    "skipped" : 0,
```

```
      "failed" : 0
    },
    "hits" : {
      "total" : {
        "value" : 1,
        "relation" : "eq"
      },
      "max_score" : 1.2039728,
      "hits" : [
        {
          "_index" : "userdetails",
          "_type" : "_doc",
          "_id" : "3",
          "_score" : 1.2039728,
          "_source" : {
            "name" : "Anurag",
            "gender" : "male",
            "city" : "New Delhi",
            "age" : 37
          }
        }
      ]
    }
}
```

We must understand that we cannot search the name as Anurag here, because in term query, the term is converted to lower case. So, it will not match the term value as Anurag. Don't worry if you're unable to understand this; we will cover this in detail in the upcoming sections.

Query versus filter

In Elasticsearch, we can use a query or filter to search the documents, but there is a difference between the query and filter. In this section, we will discuss when to use a query and when to use the filter. Generally, we use a query when we want to know how well a query clause matches the document, whereas the filter can be used to know whether a document matches the query clause exactly. In the case of a query, the relevance score is calculated based on the match, which is shown under the _score meta field. In the case of a filter, no score is calculated because it either exactly matches the term or there is no match, so there is no relevancy in case of filter. This way, we use the filter when we want to do an exact match, but we use a query when we want to perform a search where we want to see how well the search keyword matches the document.

Now, we will cover the different options that Elasticsearch provides for request body search, like query, filter, and sort. Let's start with query.

Query

Using the query keyword, we can perform the body search where we can pass the search value against the field name on which we want to search. Let's construct a query and see how we can search for any field value. In the preceding query, we did a term query search where we provided the field value in a small case. However, if we want to do the exact search, we can use the `fieldname.keyword` in which we search the exact value instead of analyzed value. Refer to the following expression:

```
GET userdetails/_search
{
  "query": {
    "term": {
      "name.keyword": {
        "value": "Atul"
      }
    }
  }
}
```

In the preceding expression, we are searching for the exact value of the name by using the `name.keyword` field instead of `name` only. This ensures that we will search for the not analyzed value instead of the analyzed value. We will get the following response from this query:

```
{
  "took" : 0,
  "timed_out" : false,
  "_shards" : {
    "total" : 1,
```

```
    "successful" : 1,
    "skipped" : 0,
    "failed" : 0
  },
  "hits" : {
    "total" : {
      "value" : 1,
      "relation" : "eq"
    },
    "max_score" : 1.2039728,
    "hits" : [
      {
        "_index" : "userdetails",
        "_type" : "_doc",
        "_id" : "4",
        "_score" : 1.2039728,
        "_source" : {
          "name" : "Amar",
          "gender" : "male",
          "city" : "Mumbai",
          "age" : 30
        }
      }
    ]
  }
}
```

In this response, we get the output by providing the exact name, that is, `Amar`. This way, we can perform a data search using a query.

Query types

As we discussed earlier, there are mainly two types of queries we can perform on Elasticsearch also along with that we have compound queries:

- **Full-text search:** In full-text search queries, we match the search text against a text field. The analyzer is used as per the field type before doing the actual search. The relevant results are returned after matching the text with the field values.

- **Term-level queries:** For term-level queries, no analysis is performed before the search, and they are used to match the exact term value against the field.

- **Compound queries:** We can join multiple simple queries to create compound queries. We can construct a complex query by joining the simple queries. In a search application, you are required to create compound queries.

Now, we will cover each of these in detail to understand how they can be used for different use cases.

Full-text search

As we mentioned earlier, analysis is performed, and it is used to match the text against the field values for full-text search based queries. We have the following query options to perform full-text search queries:

- `match_all`
- `match`
- `match_phrase`
- `multi_match`
- `query_string`

match_all

Using the `match_all` query, we can match all the documents, and it provides a great score of 1.0 to all the returned documents as we don't provide any search term. We can execute the match all query be executing the following expression:

```
GET /_search
{
    "query": {
        "match_all": {}
    }
}
```

We also have the match none query, which is the opposite of the match-all query and matches no documents. The syntax of the match none query is as follows:

```
GET /_search
{
    "query": {
        "match_none": {}
```

```
        }
}
```

This way, match all can be used if we want to match everything, and the match none query can be used if we don't want to match anything.

match

Using the match query, we can fetch matching documents for a given value, which can be text, number, boolean, or a date. In this query, the provided text is first analyzed and then matched against the field values:

```
GET userdetails/_search
{
  "query": {
    "match": {
      "name": {
        "query": "Anurag"
      }
    }
  }
}
```

In the preceding match query expression, we are trying to match the name field against the query as Anurag. It will give us the following document as the response:

```
{
        "_index" : "userdetails",
        "_type" : "_doc",
        "_id" : "3",
        "_score" : 1.2039728,
        "_source" : {
          "name" : "Anurag",
          "gender" : "male",
          "city" : "New Delhi",
          "age" : 37
        }
}
```

In the match query, we can also provide an operator like and or or. By default, the operator is or, but we can set it as follows:

```
GET userdetails/_search
{
  "query": {
    "match": {
      "name": {
        "query": "Anurag Srivastava",
        "operator": "and"
      }
    }
  }
}
```

The preceding expression will search for Anurag and Srivastava. If we don't provide the and operator, Elasticsearch will return all documents matching either with Anurag or Srivastava.

match_phrase

The match_phrase query retrieves documents with a match of a complete sentence instead of individual words. It also matches the documents with the same order of words in the search criteria. Refer to this example:

```
GET userdetails/_search
{
  "query": {
    "match_phrase": {
      "name": {
        "query": "Anurag Srivastava"
      }
    }
  }
}
```

In the preceding query, we are trying to fetch the exact name as Anurag Srivastava instead of matching the individual first name and last name in different documents. So, the preceding query will return only those documents where the name is Anurag Srivastava. Take a look at the response for the preceding query:

```
{
        "_index" : "userdetails",
        "_type" : "_doc",
        "_id" : "5",
        "_score" : 1.7770996,
        "_source" : {
          "name" : "Anurag Srivastava",
          "gender" : "male",
          "city" : "Pune",
          "age" : 39
        }
    }
}
```

This way, we can search for the exact phrase instead of individual words using the
match_phrase query.

multi_match

Using a multi_match query, we can search across multiple fields of the document.
This is suitable when we want to match something against more than a single field.
Using the preceding expression, we can execute the multi_match query:

```
GET userdetails/_search
{
  "query": {
    "multi_match": {
        "query": "Anurag Srivastava",
        "fields": ["name", "details"]
      }
  }
}
```

So, we can match something against the name and details fields using the above-
mentioned expression.

query_string

Query string provides a syntax that is parsed through a parser and can be split based
on an operator, like AND, OR, or NOT. After splitting, the text is analyzed before
matching it against the fields. We can construct a complex query using query string
as it supports wildcard characters and multi-field search. Also, multiple operators
can be used. The following expression shows a query string example:

```
GET userdetails/_search
{
  "query": {
    "query_string": {
        "query": "Anurag OR Srivastava",
        "default_field": "name"
      }
    }
}
```

In the preceding query, we are trying to search the first name and the last name using the OR operator. So, this query will return all documents that match the first name, last name, or the first name along with the last name. We have also provided the default field it should match; this field will be used if the field is not provided in the query string. We can also create groups for multiple conditions and how they should be treated. For example, look at the following example:

```
GET userdetails/_search
{
  "query": {
    "query_string": {
        "query": "(Anurag AND Srivastava) OR Amar",
        "default_field": "name"
      }
    }
}
```

Here, we are grouping the condition where the name should be Anurag Srivastava or Amar. This was just an example, and we can group these conditions similarly.

We can execute the query on multiple fields by providing the field parameter in the query. We can add more than one field in the query, as follows:

```
"fields" : ["name", "details"]
```

This example shows that we can add the name and details field using the field parameter. This way, we can do the full-text search queries. Now, let's discuss how to perform term-based queries.

Term-level queries

We have the following term-based search options, using which we can perform different term-based queries:

- Term query
- Terms query
- Exists query
- Range query
- Fuzzy query
- Wildcard query

Term query

As we discussed earlier, term queries perform the search with the exact term for a given field. Generally, we use a term query against the precise values, like for the price value, age, any id, or the username. So, we can mostly use it for non-text fields, but it is not recommended for text fields. We can use the match queries for text fields. The following expression shows a term query example:

```
GET userdetails/_search
{
  "query": {
    "term": {
      "age": {
        "value": 30
      }
    }
  }
}
```

In the preceding term query, we are fetching the users with age as 30, so it is, again, a precise numeric value well suited for a term query.

Terms query

We use the terms query to fetch the documents having one or more exact terms for the given fields. The terms query is very similar to the term query except we can search for multiple values using the terms query. The following expression is showing a terms query:

```
GET userdetails/_search
{
```

```
"query": {
  "terms": {
    "age": [30, 39]
  }
}
}
```

In the preceding terms query, we want to fetch the documents with age 30 or 39. So, you can identify the difference between the term query and terms query. In the term query, we search for a single value, whereas we can provide multiple values to search against the field using terms.

Exists query

Using the exists query, we can fetch the documents that contain the field we are looking for. As Elasticsearch is schema-less, it may be possible that the field may not exist in all documents. We can use the following expression to look for any field if it exists in the document:

```
GET userdetails/_search
{
  "query": {
    "exists": {
        "field": "gender"
    }
  }
}
```

Using the preceding query, we are fetching the documents where the gender field exists. It is important to fetch those documents where a certain field is available.

Range query

Using the range query, we can fetch the documents that contain the field values within a given range, like fetching all documents where the age is between 30 and 35 years. The following expression provides an example of a range query:

```
GET userdetails/_search
{
  "query": {
    "range" : {
        "age" : { "gte" : 30, "lte" : 35 }
```

```
        }
    }
}
```

The preceding expression shows a range query where we are fetching all the documents with the age range between 30 and 35. We can also apply range on other fields like price, date, or quantity.

Fuzzy query

Using a fuzzy query, we can fetch the documents that are similar to the search term, and a Levenshtein edit distance measures that similarity. The Levenshtein distance is a string metric, using which we can measure the difference between two sequences. The edit distance is calculated based on the number of changes required for one character to turn one term into another. An example is to convert cat into a rat by changing c to r. Refer to the following example:

```
GET userdetails/_search
{
  "query": {
    "fuzzy": {
      "name": {
        "value": "ama"
      }
    }
  }
}
```

The preceding expression shows a fuzzy query where we are trying to search the name with text ama. This will return all the documents where a single-character modification can match the value with any field. This modification can be character replacement, addition, deletion, or transposing two adjacent characters. After executing the preceding command, we can get the following response:

```
    {
        "_index" : "userdetails",
        "_type" : "_doc",
        "_id" : "4",
        "_score" : 0.9918202,
        "_source" : {
          "name" : "Amar",
```

```
        "gender" : "male",
        "city" : "Mumbai",
        "age" : 30
    }
}
```

The query returns the preceding response with the name Amar as it matches the search word ama. This way, we can construct the fuzzy query as per our requirement.

Wildcard query

Using a wildcard query, we can provide a wildcard pattern to fetch the documents that match the wildcard pattern. We can provide the wildcard operator to match zero or more characters. Take a look at this expression:

```
GET userdetails/_search
{
  "query": {
    "wildcard": {
      "name": {
        "value": "a*g"
      }
    }
  }
}
```

Here, we are using the wildcard query to match the name that starts with a and ends with g. After executing the preceding query, we will get the following response:

```
{
        "_index" : "userdetails",
        "_type" : "_doc",
        "_id" : "3",
        "_score" : 1.0,
        "_source" : {
          "name" : "Anurag",
          "gender" : "male",
          "city" : "New Delhi",
          "age" : 37
```

```
      }
   }
```

This result is based on the wildcard query where we have mentioned a*g. We can adjust the wildcard query as per our requirement, like we can skip the last character to match all names that start with the character a. This way, we can apply the wildcard queries to fetch the documents using the provided pattern.

Compound queries

In Elasticsearch, we create the query clauses to perform search operations. These are good for performing simple search operations, but we can perform complex search operations by combining these query clauses. This can be done by combining the query JSON structure. These Elasticsearch clauses can be of two types: leaf clauses and compound clauses. In a leaf clause, we generally search a keyword against the index, so it is quite simple in structure. On the other hand, we combine different clauses in compound clauses.

Boolean query

In a Boolean query, we combine other queries through Boolean operators to fetch the matching documents. We have different occurrence types in a Boolean query:

- must: The matching documents must match the clause.
- should: The matching documents should match the clause.
- must_not: The matching documents must not match the clause.
- filter: The clause must appear in the matching documents. The only difference is that must impacts the score, while filter does not.

We can use the bool keyword to combine different clauses; refer to the given example:

```
POST _search
{
   "query": {
      "bool" : {
         "must" : {
            "term" : { "name" : "anurag" }
         },
         "must_not" : {
            "range" : {
               "age" : { "gte" : 10, "lte" : 20 }
            }
```

```
        },
        "should" : [
          { "term" : { "gender" : "male" } }
        ]
      }
    }
}
```

In the preceding expression, we created a compound clause where we want to fetch the documents with name as anurag, gender as male, and the age not in the range of 10 to 20 years. This way, we can construct compound queries, and we will get the following response after executing the preceding expression:

```
{
  "took" : 5,
  "timed_out" : false,
  "_shards" : {
    "total" : 27,
    "successful" : 27,
    "skipped" : 0,
    "failed" : 0
  },
  "hits" : {
    "total" : {
      "value" : 1,
      "relation" : "eq"
    },
    "max_score" : 1.5606477,
    "hits" : [
      {
        "_index" : "userdetails",
        "_type" : "_doc",
        "_id" : "3",
        "_score" : 1.5606477,
        "_source" : {
          "name" : "Anurag",
```

```
            "gender" : "male",
            "city" : "New Delhi",
            "age" : 37
        }
      }
    ]
  }
}
```

This way, we can combine different clauses and can perform a complex Boolean search.

Boosting query

The boosting query can be used to fetch the documents that match the positive query, but it reduces the relevance score of the document if it matches the negative query. In a boosting query, we provide the positive and negative matching criteria to affect the relevance score. Refer to the example given here:

```
GET userdetails/_search
{
    "query": {
        "boosting" : {
            "positive" : {
                "term" : {
                    "name": "anurag"
                }
            },
            "negative" : {
                "term" : {
                    "city" : "Pune"
                }
            },
            "negative_boost" : 0.5
        }
    }
}
```

Here, we have given the criteria for positive and negative conditions. In the positive case, we want to match the documents with the name anurag, while we want to affect the score in the negative case with the condition where the city name is Pune. After executing the preceding query, we will get the following response:

```
"hits" : [
    {
        "_index" : "userdetails",
        "_type" : "_doc",
        "_id" : "3",
        "_score" : 0.9395274,
        "_source" : {
            "name" : "Anurag",
            "gender" : "male",
            "city" : "New Delhi",
            "age" : 37
        }
    },
    {
        "_index" : "userdetails",
        "_type" : "_doc",
        "_id" : "5",
        "_score" : 0.68786836,
        "_source" : {
            "name" : "Anurag Srivastava",
            "gender" : "male",
            "city" : "Pune",
            "age" : 39
        }
    }
]
```

In the response, we can see that the score of the document having the city like Pune is 0.687, while the other city scores are 0.939.

Multi-search

We can perform a multi-search on Elasticsearch using the multi-search API or multi search template. Using multi-search, we can provide multiple search queries in a single hit to Elasticsearch. The structure of a multi-search is as follows:

```
header\n
body\n
header\n
body\n
```

Using the preceding structure, we can provide multiple queries. Now, let's see how this can be done using the multi-search API and template.

Multi-search API

Using the multi-search API, we can perform several searches in a single API request. Refer to the following example for performing multiple searches:

```
GET userdetails/_msearch
{ }
{"query" : {"match" : { "name": "anurag"}}}
{"index": "kibana_sample_data_ecommerce"}
{"query" : {"match" : {"customer_first_name" : "George" }}}
```

Using the preceding expression, we are searching for data across multiple indices in a single API hit. In the first search, we are fetching documents with name as `anurag` from the `userdetails` index and the documents with `customer_first_name` as George from the next index `kibana_sample_data_ecommerce`. This way, we can search multiple indices in a single hit.

Multi search template

The multi-search template is similar to the multi-search API, as they follow the same structure. The only difference is that the multi-search template supports file, stored, and inline templates. Refer to the following example:

```
$ cat multisearch
{"index": "userdetails"}
{"source": {"query": {"match": {"user" : "{{username}}" }}}, "params": {"username": "anurag"}}
{"source": {"query": {"{{query_type}}": {"name": "{{name}}" }}},
```

```
"params": {"query_type": "match_phrase_prefix", "name": "Anurag
Srivastava"}}
{"index": "_all"}
{"id": "template_1", "params": {"query_string": "search for these words"
}}


$ curl -H "Content-Type: application/x-ndjson" -XGET localhost:9200/_
msearch/template --data-binary "@multisearch"; echo
```

Here, we can create a file and pass it in the CURL request to search the documents.

Explain API

The explain API explains the score for the query and documents. It provides us with information on why the query is matching or not matching specific documents. Here, we must provide the document id as a parameter, as the explain query provides the explanation of whether it is matching or not matching using this ID.

```
GET userdetails/_explain/3
{
  "query": {
    "match": {
      "name": "anurag"
      }
  }
}
```

In the preceding query, 3 is the id of the document matching the given query, and we have taken this id to understand how this document was matched with the given query.

Profile API

We can use the Profile API for debugging, as it provides details on execution timing for individual components for a search request. Using this API, we can get the details on why some requests are slow, and we can improve the performance using that information. In any search request, we can enable the profiling by adding a top-level profile parameter. The following expression provides an example of the Profile API:

```
GET userdetails/_search
{
```

```
    "profile": true,
  "query": {
    "match": {
      "name": {
        "query": "anurag"
      }
    }
  }
}
```

After executing the preceding command, we can get the profiling details along with the query results, as follows:

```
"profile" : {
    "shards" : [
      {
        "id" : "[OsuaWgbGQd2KXbWE3ENfEg][userdetails][0]",
        "searches" : [
          {
            "query" : [
              {
                "type" : "TermQuery",
                "description" : "name:anurag",
                "time_in_nanos" : 1354098,
                "breakdown" : {
                  "set_min_competitive_score_count" : 0,
                  "match_count" : 0,
                  "shallow_advance_count" : 0,
                  "set_min_competitive_score" : 0,
                  "next_doc" : 7040,
                  "match" : 0,
                  "next_doc_count" : 2,
                  "score_count" : 2,
                  "compute_max_score_count" : 0,
                  "compute_max_score" : 0,
```

```
                              "advance" : 9356,
                              "advance_count" : 2,
                              "score" : 17092,
                              "build_scorer_count" : 7,
                              "create_weight" : 100601,
                              "shallow_advance" : 0,
                              "create_weight_count" : 1,
                              "build_scorer" : 1219995
                          }
                      }
                  ],
                  "rewrite_time" : 9183,
                  "collector" : [
                      {
                          "name" : "SimpleTopScoreDocCollector",
                          "reason" : "search_top_hits",
                          "time_in_nanos" : 55470
                      }
                  ]
              }
          ],
          "aggregations" : [ ]
      }
    ]
  }
}
```

In the preceding profile result, we can see different details that we will understand here:

- Under the shards section, we can see the shard ids that were used in the response.
- Then, we have a query section under searches, which contains the details for the execution of the query.
- Under query, we have a breakdown section that shows the execution statistics of low-level Lucene queries.

- For each query, we have the rewrite time, which represents the cumulative rewrite time.

- We have a collector section that tells about the Lucene collectors, using which the search was executed.

- Then, we have the aggregation section that tells us about the execution of aggregation.

This way, we can use the Profile API to get the details for query execution, like the timing of individual query components. We can also identify why the query is slow and can tweak it to improve performance.

Conclusion

In this chapter, we understood how to perform data search. We started with the URI search and then covered the request body search. Then, we looked at the difference between query and filter and different query types, like full-text search, term-level queries, and compound queries. Then, we explored multi-search, where we discussed the multi-search API and multi-search template. At the end, we walked through the explain API and profile API, using which we can get the query details and can improve performance.

In the next chapter, we will discuss the geo queries and how we can handle geodata. We will also learn about geo data types and how we can create geo-mapping. Additionally, we will see how to add and search geodata in Elasticsearch.

Questions

1. What is an empty search?

2. How can we perform the URI field search?

3. What is the difference between query and filter?

4. What is the difference between `match_phrase` and match query?

5. What is a fuzzy query? Give an example of the fuzzy query.

6. What is a wildcard query? Give an example of the wildcard query.

## CHAPTER 8

Handling Geo with Elasticsearch

Introduction

In the last chapter, we discussed data search using URI and request body search. Under body search, we covered the query and filter and the difference between the two. We also explored the full-text search, term-level queries, and compound queries. We got to know about multi-search and how to perform multi-search using API and template. Additionally, we understood how to get the query details using the explain and profile APIs. In this chapter, we will look at how to manage geospatial data. We will learn how to save geodata in Elasticsearch and how to perform geo queries. Geospatial data search is required when we want to perform an operation based on geo locations, like the nearest cab search, nearest restaurant search, and such.

Using Elasticsearch, we can handle location-based data for multiple use cases, like querying within the given radius, sorting the records based on the location, data aggregation based on location, and such. These days, many of our day-to-day activities are dependent on location-based data search, like the cab service for transportation. The accuracy of in-cab location is the key for an efficient service operation. Similarly, food apps use the location search to deliver food from the nearest restaurants. Grocery apps also use location data search for delivering groceries to customers. In this mobile age, everything is somehow dependent on location; users should get things as per their current location. Elasticsearch geodata handling is well suited for these use cases, and it helps such businesses. Elasticsearch provides us with the feature to perform these geo queries on geodata after storing the location-based data.

Structure

In this chapter, we will cover the following:

- Geodata type
- Geo point data
- Geo shape data
- Geo queries
- Use case

Objective

After studying this unit, you should be able to:

- Understand different geodata types
- Create the mappings for the geodata
- Add and search geo data in Elasticsearch

Geodata type

Although Elasticsearch creates a dynamic mapping for many data types, we have to create the mapping for the geo types explicitly. In Elasticsearch, we have two ways to represent geodata:

- **geo-point:** We use it to store data in the form of latitude-longitude pairs in case of the geo-point.
- **Geo-shape:** We use it to store complex shapes, which are defined in the form of GeoJSON in case of geo-shape. These shapes include circle, polygon, and such.

Now, let's discuss these types in detail and understand how to save the data of each type in Elasticsearch, and then we will move on to searching that data.

Geo point data

The Elasticsearch `geo_point` data type accepts latitude and longitude pairs and can save them in different ways, which we will discuss in detail. Using this `geo_point` data, we can do a lot of things. The following points list some of the features of `geo_point` data:

- We can fetch the points within a range from a central point.
- We can find the geo-points within a box or polygon.

- We can aggregate the documents through distance through a central point.
- We can use the distance for the relevancy score of the document.
- We can use the distance for sorting the documents.

These were some of the features of geo-point data. Now, let's see how we can save the geo-point data.

Creating mapping

As we discussed earlier, we must explicitly create the mapping for geodata types; so, let's create the mapping for the `geo_point` data by writing the following expression:

```
PUT geo_index
{
  "mappings": {
    "properties": {
      "location": {
        "type": "geo_point"
      }
    }
  }
}
```

This way, we can create the mapping of `geo_point` data type for the field location in the index named `geo_index`. Ideally, we will create the `geo_index` index, where the field name location is mapped with the `geo_point` type. After executing the preceding command, we will get the following response:

```
{
  "acknowledged" : true,
  "shards_acknowledged" : true,
  "index" : "geo_index"
}
```

This way, we can create the `geo_point` data type mapping. Once the mapping is created, we can start saving documents in the index.

Saving geo point data

In Elaticsearch, there are different ways to save the geo-point data, and we can use any method. There are a total of five different ways to save the geo-point data:

- **As an object:** We can save the geo-point data in the form of an object. Refer to the following example:

```
POST geo_index/_doc
{
  "text": "Object type Geo-point data",
  "location": {
    "lat": 42.14,
    "lon": -73.46
  }
}
```

Using this expression, we can save the geodata in the form of an object.

- **As a string:** The geodata can also be saved in the form of a string, where the latitude and longitude are saved in the form of a string. Take a look at this example:

```
POST geo_index/_doc
{
  "text": "String type Geo-point data",
  "location": "42.14,-73.46"
}
```

Here, we are saving the location field data in the form of a string.

- **Geohash:** We can save the geo-point data in the form of geohash, which is a short alphanumeric string representation of the latitude and longitude combination. Geohash provides us with a way to conveniently represent the location through a short alphanumeric string form. Refer to this expression:

```
POST geo_index/_doc
{
  "text": "Geohash type Geo-point data",
  "location": "gbsuv7ztq"
}
```

This way, we can create the document using the geohash type location.

- **As an array:** The geodata can also be saved in the form of an array, where the latitude and longitude are saved in the form of an array. Look at the following example:

```
POST geo_index/_doc
{
    "text": "Array type Geo-point data",
    "location": [ -73.46, 42.14 ]
}
```

This way, we can save the geo-point data in the form of an array. In the case of an array, the longitude comes before the latitude.

- **Point:** The geo-point data can also be saved using a well-known text point format, where we use the format as POINT(lon lan). Here's an example:

```
POST geo_index/_doc
{
    "text": "Point type Geo-point data",
    "location":"POINT (-73.46 42.14)"
}
```

This way, we can save the location data using the point representation.

Geo shape data

Using the geo_shape data type, we can index and search arbitrary geo shapes, which can be a rectangular shape, polygons, or circle. When we have a requirement where we need to index or search the shapes instead of point location, we can use the geo_shape data type of Elasticsearch. It has the following shape types:

- **Point:** This is a single point with latitude and longitude, or we can say a single geographic coordinate.

- **LineString:** LineString is an arbitrary line between two or more points that can be defined in the form of an array representing two or more positions.

- **Polygon:** Polygon is represented as a closed shape where the first and the last point should match. So, if we want to create a polygon with n sides, it should have n+1 vertices. A list of points defines a polygon shape.

- **MultiPoint:** A MultiPoint is a shape type having related points that are not connected. A MultiPoint shape can also be represented as an array.

- **MultiLineString:** A MultiLineString is a combination of LineString, where it can be represented using an array of different linestrings.

- **MultiPolygon:** A MultiPolygon is also a group of polygons that we can represent in the form of an array.

- **GeometryCollection:** This can be represented as a geojson collection of geometry objects.

- **Envelope:** An Envelope shape can be represented with two points, that is the top left and bottom right points of the shape.

- **Circle:** A Circle shape can be defined by providing the centre point, along with the radius with the unit. The default unit is METERS.

These are some geo shape types using which we can save the geodata in Elasticsearch. Now, we will look at how to create the mapping for these geo shape types in Elasticsearch.

Creating mapping

We must create the mapping in Elasticsearch explicitly for any shape type, and the same is the case for Geo-shape. Let's see how we can create the mapping for the Geo-shape data. We must write the following expression to create the Geo-shape mapping in Elasticsearch:

```
PUT geoshape_index
{
  "mappings": {
    "properties": {
      "location": {
        "type": "geo_shape"
      }
    }
  }
}
```

This way, we can create the mapping of geo_shape data type for the field location in the index named geoshape_index. Ideally, we will create the geoshape_index index, where the field name location is mapped with the geo_shape type. After executing the above-mentioned command, we will get the following response:

```
{
  "acknowledged" : true,
  "shards_acknowledged" : true,
  "index" : "geoshape_index"
}
```

This response shows that the command is executed successfully, and the `geoshape_index` index is created with the `geo_shape` data type mapping with the location field. This way, we can create the `geo_shape` data type mapping. Once the mapping is created, we can start saving documents in the index.

Saving geo point data

Now, we will see how these shapes can be created in Elasticsearch, but we must first understand that the shapes can be represented in two formats: GeoJSON and Well-known Text (WKT) format. So, we will explain both ways to map these shapes in Elasticsearch. Let's explore the different Geo-shape types and how to save documents in each type.

Point

As discussed earlier, a single geographic coordinate is used to represent the point geo type. If we want to save the document for the point type in the GeoJSON format, we need to execute the following expression:

```
POST geoshape_index/_doc
{
  "text": "Point type Geo-shape data",
  "location": {
      "type" : "point",
      "coordinates" : [-73.03, 42.89]
    }
}
```

Using this expression, we can create a document of geo point type using GeoJSON. On the other hand, if we want to create the geo point type document using Well-known Text (WKT) format, we need to write the following expression:

```
POST geoshape_index/_doc
{
  "text": "Point type Geo-shape data",
  "location": "POINT (-73.46 42.14)"
}
```

We can save the point type geo data using the WKT format using this expression.

LineString

Two or more positions define a LineString shape, and we use to represent it in the form of an array. If we specify only two points, it will generate a straight line by joining those two points. However, if we specify more than two points, it will generate an arbitrary path. If we want to create a LineString using GeoJSON, we need to execute the following command:

```
POST geoshape_index/_doc
{
  "text": "LineString type Geo-shape data",
  "location":{
      "type" : "linestring",
      "coordinates" : [[-78.03653, 36.897676], [-78.009051,
36.889939]]
    }
}
```

Using the preceding expression, we can save the LineString in the GeoJSON format. We can save the LineString in the WKT format with the following expression:

```
POST geoshape_index/_doc
{
  "text": "LineString type Geo-shape data",
  "location" : "LINESTRING (-77.03653 38.897676, -77.009051 38.889939)"
}
```

With this, we can save the LineString type geo shape data using the WKT format.

Polygon

Polygon is a closed shape, where the first and the last point should match. So, if we want to create a polygon with n sides, it should have n+1 vertices. A list of points defines a polygon shape. We can save the Polygon shape with GeoJSON using the following expression:

```
POST geoshape_index/_doc
{
  "text": "Polygon type Geo-shape data",
  "location":{
      "type" : "polygon",
```

```
      "coordinates" : [
            [ [100.0, 0.0], [101.0, 0.0], [101.0, 1.0], [100.0, 1.0],
[100.0, 0.0] ]
         ]
      }
}
```

The preceding expression can be used to save the Polygon in the GeoJSON format. Now, we can save the Polygon in the WKT format using the following expression:

```
POST geoshape_index/_doc
{
    "text": "Polygon type Geo-shape data",
    "location" : "POLYGON ((100.0 0.0, 101.0 0.0, 101.0 1.0, 100.0 1.0,
100.0 0.0))"
}
```

With the preceding expression, we can save the Polygon type geo shape data using the WKT format. We can also create a Polygon with a hole by defining the outer and inner boundary, where the outer boundary will form the outer layer, while the inner boundary will form the actual hole. Refer to the expression given here, using which we can create the Polygon with hole:

```
POST geoshape_index/_doc
{
    "text": "Polygon with a hole using GeoJSON",
    "location":{
        "type" : "polygon",
        "coordinates" : [
            [ [100.0, 0.0], [101.0, 0.0], [101.0, 1.0], [100.0, 1.0],
[100.0, 0.0] ],
            [ [100.2, 0.2], [100.8, 0.2], [100.8, 0.8], [100.2, 0.8],
[100.2, 0.2] ]
        ]
    }
}
```

Using this expression, we can create the Polygon with a hole through GeoJSON. If we want to create the Polygon with a hole through WKT, we need to execute the following expression:

```
POST geoshape_index/_doc
{
  "text": "Polygon with a hole using WKT",
  "location" : "POLYGON ((100.0 0.0, 101.0 0.0, 101.0 1.0, 100.0 1.0,
100.0 0.0), (100.2 0.2, 100.8 0.2, 100.8 0.8, 100.2 0.8, 100.2 0.2))"
}
```

MultiPoint

MultiPoint is a combination of related points that are not connected. We can create the list of geojson points using the following expression:

```
POST geoshape_index/_doc
{
  "text": "Multipoint using GeoJSON",
  "location":{
      "type" : "multipoint",
      "coordinates" :[
          [102.0, 2.0], [103.0, 2.0]
      ]
   }
}
```

Using the preceding expression, we can save the MultiPoint shape through GeoJSON. If we want to save the MultiPoint shape through WKT, we need to execute the following expression:

```
POST geoshape_index/_doc
{
  "text": "Multipoint using WKT",
  "location" : "MULTIPOINT (102.0 2.0, 103.0 2.0)"
}
```

We can save the MultiPoint type geo shape data using the WKT format using the preceding expression.

MultiLineString

Multilinestring is a combination of multiple linestrings where we use an array of linestrings to represent the Multilinestring. We can save the Multilinestring using the following expression:

```
POST geoshape_index/_doc
{
  "text": "Multilinestring using GeoJSON",
  "location":{
      "type" : "multilinestring",
      "coordinates" :[
          [ [102.0, 2.0], [103.0, 2.0], [103.0, 3.0], [102.0, 3.0] ],
          [ [100.0, 0.0], [101.0, 0.0], [101.0, 1.0], [100.0, 1.0] ],
          [ [100.2, 0.2], [100.8, 0.2], [100.8, 0.8], [100.2, 0.8] ]
      ]
  }
}
```

Using the preceding expression, we can save the Multilinestring shape through GeoJSON. If we want to save the Multilinestring shape through WKT, we need to execute the following expression:

```
POST geoshape_index/_doc
{
  "text": "Multilinestring using WKT",
  "location" : "MULTILINESTRING ((102.0 2.0, 103.0 2.0, 103.0 3.0, 102.0
3.0), (100.0 0.0, 101.0 0.0, 101.0 1.0, 100.0 1.0), (100.2 0.2, 100.8
0.2, 100.8 0.8, 100.2 0.8))"
}
```

Using the preceding expression, we can save the Multilinestring type geo shape data using the WKT format.

MultiPolygon

A MultiPolygon is a group of polygons that we can represent in the form of an array. We can use the following expression to create a MultiPolygon using a list of geojson polygons:

```
POST geoshape_index/_doc/12
{
  "text": "MultiPolygon using GeoJSON",
  "location":{
      "type" : "multipolygon",
```

```
        "coordinates" : [
                [ [[102.0, 2.0], [103.0, 2.0], [103.0, 3.0], [102.0, 3.0],
[102.0, 2.0]] ],
                [ [[100.0, 0.0], [101.0, 0.0], [101.0, 1.0], [100.0, 1.0],
[100.0, 0.0]],
                    [[100.2, 0.2], [100.8, 0.2], [100.8, 0.8], [100.2, 0.8],
[100.2, 0.2]] ]
            ]
        }
}
```

Using this expression, we can save the MultiPolygon shape through GeoJSON. If we want to save the MultiPolygon shape through WKT, we must execute the following expression:

```
POST geoshape_index/_doc
{
  "text": "MultiPolygon using WKT",
  "location" : "MULTIPOLYGON (((102.0 2.0, 103.0 2.0, 103.0 3.0, 102.0
3.0, 102.0 2.0)), ((100.0 0.0, 101.0 0.0, 101.0 1.0, 100.0 1.0, 100.0
0.0), (100.2 0.2, 100.8 0.2, 100.8 0.8, 100.2 0.8, 100.2 0.2)))"
}
```

Using the above expression, we can save the MultiPolygon type geo shape data using the WKT format.

Geometry collection

A GeometryCollection can be represented as geojson collection of geometry objects. The below expression is showing the example of a collection of geojson geometry objects:

```
POST geoshape_index/_doc
{
  "text": " GeometryCollection using GeoJSON",
  "location" : {
        "type": "geometrycollection",
        "geometries": [
            {
                "type": "point",
```

```
            "coordinates": [100.0, 0.0]
        },
        {
            "type": "linestring",
            "coordinates": [ [101.0, 0.0], [102.0, 1.0] ]
        }
    ]
}
}
```

Using the following expression, we can save the GeometryCollection shape through GeoJSON. If we want to save the GeometryCollection shape through WKT, we need to execute the following expression:

```
POST geoshape_index/_doc
{
    "text": " GeometryCollection using WKT",
    "location" : "GEOMETRYCOLLECTION (POINT (100.0 0.0), LINESTRING
(101.0 0.0, 102.0 1.0))"
}
```

Using the preceding expression, we can save the GeometryCollection type geo shape data using the WKT format.

Envelope

An Envelope shape can be represented with two points: the top left and bottom right points of the shape. We can represent the envelope boundary in the [[minLon, maxLat][maxLon, minLat]] format, which forms the structure of the envelope. We can represent the Envelop shape in geojson using the following expression:

```
POST geoshape_index/_doc
{
  "text": "Envelope using GeoJSON",
   "location" : {
        "type" : "envelope",
        "coordinates" : [ [100.0, 1.0], [101.0, 0.0] ]
   }
}
```

Using the preceding expression, we can save the Envelope shape through GeoJSON. If we want to save the Envelope shape through WKT, we need to execute the following expression:

```
POST geoshape_index/_doc
{
  "text": "Envelope using WKT",
  "location" : "BBOX (100.0, 102.0, 2.0, 0.0)"
}
```

In WKT specification, we saved the Envelope shape in the following order: `minLon, maxLat, maxLat, minLat`. Using the preceding expression, we can save the Envelope type geo shape data using the WKT format.

Circle

A Circle shape can be defined by providing the centre point, along with the radius with the unit. The default unit is METERS. A circle type is neither a GeoJSON nor a WKT structure, and we can save the circle data using the following expression:

```
POST geoshape_index/_doc
{
  "text": "Circle data",
   "location" : {
        "type" : "circle",
        "coordinates" : [101.0, 1.0],
        "radius" : "100m"
    }
}
```

Using the preceding expression, we can save the Circle type geo shape data. Till now, we covered how to create mapping and add documents for geodata. Let's move to exploring how we can perform the search operation on geodata.

Geo queries

As we discussed earlier, Elasticsearch has two types of geodata support: `geo_point` and `geo_shape`. The `geo_point` is used when we want to save the latitude and longitude from specifying a single point, while the `geo_shape` can be used to support various shapes like line, circle, and polygons. Now, if we want to search the geodata, Elasticsearch supports the following types of queries:

- geo_distance query: Here, we can find the documents with geo points that range for a given distance from a central point.
- geo_polygon query: Here, we can query the documents with geo points that range within a given polygon structure.
- geo_bounding_box query: Here, we find the documents whose geo points range against a given rectangle.
- geo_shape query: The geo_shape query fetches a document if it has the shape that intersects the query shape using the geo_shape mapping grid square representation.

These are some geo query types, using which we can perform the geo queries on different types of geodata. Let's cover each of them in detail.

Geo-distance queries

We use the geo-distance queries to find out the documents within a specific range from a geo point. For example, if we want to know the ATM within a range of 5 KM from our location, we can perform the geo-distance based queries. We can execute these queries by providing the distance filter, along with other condition if required, or we can simply run a match all query and put the distance filter. Refer to the following expression:

```
GET /geo_index/_search
{
    "query": {
        "bool" : {
            "must" : {
                "match_all" : {}
            },
            "filter" : {
                "geo_distance" : {
                    "distance" : "100km",
                    "location" : {
                        "lat" : 42,
                        "lon" : -73
                    }
                }
            }
        }
    }
}
```

```
        }
}
```

Here, we are providing a filter condition where we want to fetch all the documents in a range of 100 KM radius from the given lat lon for the location. Similarly, we can execute this query for any distance from the lat lon and fetch the documents with the lat lon that occurs in the given distance range.

The distance in geo-distance queries supports different units, and some of the units we can use are as follows:

- **Mile:** mi or miles
- **Yard:** yd or yards
- **Kilometer:** km or kilometers
- **Meter:** m or meters
- **Centimeter:** cm or centimeters
- **Millimeter:** mm or millimeters
- **Nautical mile:** NM, nmi, or nauticalmiles
- **Feet:** ft or feet
- **Inch:** in or inch

We can use any unit for the geo-distance search as we have used km for searching in a range of 100 kilometers.

Geo-distance-based queries are based on geo-point, so they support all different geo point representations of the location. The distance filter supports all those geo-point location types that we covered during document creation, and they can be represented in the following ways:

Lat Long as properties: Here, we represent the location with individual lat and lon property values. Here's an example:

```
location: {
    "lat": 42,
    "lon": -73
}
```

Lat Long as an array: Here, we represent the location in the form of an array. As discussed earlier, in array representation, we write the lon before the lat value. Refer to this example:

```
location: [-73, 42]
```

Lat Long as a string: Here, we represent the location in the form of a string. Refer to the following example:

```
location: "42,-73"
```

Lat Long as Geohash: Geohash provides us with a way to conveniently represent the location through a short alphanumeric string form. Take a look at the following expression:

```
location: "gbsuv7ztq"
```

This way, we can use any representation of the location field and perform the geo-distance based queries. These queries are frequently used for different use cases, like if we want to fetch the nearest cabs, cinema halls, ATM, or anything else. These queries can help us find those things as per the distance range provided. Now, let's see how a geo-polygon query is performed.

Geo-polygon queries

In a geo-polygon query, documents that fall within a polygon of points are fetched. The following example shows the query for a geo-polygon search:

```
GET /_search
{
    "query": {
        "bool" : {
            "must" : {
                "match_all" : {}
            },
            "filter" : {
                "geo_polygon" : {
                    "location" : {
                        "points" : [
                            {"lat" : 78, "lon" : 32},
                            {"lat" : 82, "lon" : 36},
                            {"lat" : 79, "lon" : 38}
                        ]
                    }
                }
            }
        }
```

```
          }
      }
}
```

Using this geo-polygon query, we can search the documents. The distance filter can be represented in the following ways:

Lat Long as an array: We can use the lat long value as an array, as in this expression:

```
"location" : {
      "points" : [
                [-70, 40],
                [-80, 30],
                [-90, 20]
            ]
      }
```

Lat Long as an string: We can use the lat long value as a string, as shown in this expression:

```
"location" : {
      "points" : [
                "-70, 40",
                "-80, 30",
                "-90, 20"
            ]
      }
```

Lat Long as Geohash: Geohash provides us with a way to conveniently represent the location through a short alphanumeric string form. Refer to the following expression:

```
"location" : {
       "points" : [
"gbsuv7ztq",
"-80, 30",
"-90, 20"
            ]
      }
```

This way, we can use any of the lat long representations for the query.

Geo-bounding box queries

In the geo-bounding query, we search the documents with the point location that is inside the bounding box, which can be specified in the search query. Here's an example:

```
GET geo_index/_search
{
    "query": {
        "bool" : {
            "must" : {
                "match_all" : {}
            },
            "filter" : {
                "geo_bounding_box" : {
                    "location" : {
                        "top_left" : {
                            "lat" : 43,
                            "lon" : -74
                        },
                        "bottom_right" : {
                            "lat" : 42,
                            "lon" : -73
                        }
                    }
                }
            }
        }
    }
}
```

Using the above-mentioned expression, we can perform the geo-bounding box query. After executing the preceding query, we will get four documents that we have added in the point type data. The following response shows a single document:

```
{
        "_index" : "geo_index",
```

```
    "_type" : "_doc",
    "_id" : "1kt78HEBL3C-ByPYREFx",
    "_score" : 1.0,
    "_source" : {
      "text" : "Object type Geo-point data",
      "location" : {
        "lat" : 42.14,
        "lon" : -73.46
      }
    }
  }
}
```

The distance filter in a geo-bounding box query can be represented as follows:

Lat Long as properties:

```
"location": {
      "top_left": {
            "lat": 40.73,
            "lon": -74.1
      },
      "bottom_right": {
            "lat": 40.01,
            "lon": -71.12
      }
}
```

Lat Long as an array:

```
"location": {
      "top_left": [-74.1, 40.73],
      "bottom_right": [-71.12, 40.01]
}
```

Lat Long as a string:

```
"location": {
      "top_left": "40.73, -74.1",
      "bottom_right": "40.01, -71.12"
}
```

Lat Long as Geohash:

```
"location": {
        "top_left": "dr5r9ydj2y73",
        "bottom_right": "drj7teegpus6"
}
```

This way, we can use any of the lat long representations for the geo-bounding box query.

Geo-shape queries

Using the geo-shape query, we can search the documents with geo-shape mapping. Here, we can fetch all those documents with a shape that intersects the query shape. Take a look at the following query, where we are trying to match with the envelope coordinates:

```
GET /geoshape_index/_search
{
    "query":{
        "bool": {
            "must": {
                "match_all": {}
            },
            "filter": {
                "geo_shape": {
                    "location": {
                        "shape": {
                            "type": "envelope",
                            "coordinates" : [[100, 1.0], [102, 0.0]]
                        },
                        "relation": "within"
                    }
                }
            }
        }
    }
}
```

This way, we can execute the geo-shape query by providing the shape coordinates in the query.

Use case

There are many use cases of geo search, and we cannot cover them all; most of them are dependent on geo search based on distance. Here, we try to search the documents ranging in between the radius of an origin point with the provided distance; for example, if I am standing at a point and want to search for the restaurants within 2 KM from my location. Ideally, we want to search all the documents from the restaurant index of Elasticsearch where the lat long of the document is in 2 KM range from my current lat-long. Now, this distance of 2 KM is a variable here, which I can change; for example, if I am unable to find any good restaurant in that range, I can increase that range to 5 KM.

That was an example of a restaurant, and we can think of other use cases like the cab aggregator service, where the app picks our current location and shows us the nearest cabs that can come to us after a successful booking. We cannot book a cab if it is far away from our location, so it needs the user's location, as all other functionality works based on that.

Restaurant search

Let's take an example where we add some documents: one for the user location and others for the nearby restaurants. We will save the following coordinates for that:

A user Location: 28.580116, 77.051673

Restaurant 1:   28.594817, 77.046608

Restaurant 2   28.593168, 77.041244

Restaurant 3   28.601345, 77.026352

Restaurant 4   28.590606, 77.062959

Now, we will first create an index named restaurants and add these restaurant coordinates. Once these are added there, we will perform the search. First, create the index with geo-point mapping by executing the following command:

```
PUT restaurants
{
  "mappings": {
    "properties": {
      "location": {
        "type": "geo_point"
      }
    }
```

```
    }
}
```

With this, we are creating the `restaurant's` index with geo-point mapping. Then, we will add the four restaurant location coordinates with their names with the following command:

```
POST restaurants/_doc
{
  "name": "Restaurant 1",
  "location": "28.594817, 77.046608"
}
```

The preceding command shows the document creation command for the first restaurant, and we can create all four restaurants in the same way. After executing the preceding command, we can get the following response:

```
{
  "_index" : "restaurants",
  "_type" : "_doc",
  "_id" : "8EvB-XEBL3C-ByPYIkGW",
  "_version" : 1,
  "result" : "created",
  "_shards" : {
    "total" : 2,
    "successful" : 1,
    "failed" : 0
  },
  "_seq_no" : 0,
  "_primary_term" : 1
}
```

After creating all the restaurant documents, we can verify them by executing the following command:

```
GET restaurants/_search
```

This command will list all the documents of the restaurant's index, and we can verify if all four restaurant documents are created in the index.

We have four restaurants with different location coordinates in our index, which we have verified. Now, we will perform the restaurant search by providing our current location and see how Elasticsearch responds to the distance queries. Now, first of all, let's see whether there is any restaurant within 1 KM range from my current location (28.580116, 77.051673) by executing the following command:

```
GET restaurants/_search
{
    "query": {
        "bool" : {
            "must" : {
                "match_all" : {}
            },
            "filter" : {
                "geo_distance" : {
                    "distance" : "1km",
                    "location" : "28.580116, 77.051673"
                }
            }
        }
    }
}
```

After executing the preceding command, we will get the following response:

```
{
  "took" : 6,
  "timed_out" : false,
  "_shards" : {
    "total" : 1,
    "successful" : 1,
    "skipped" : 0,
    "failed" : 0
  },
  "hits" : {
    "total" : {
```

```
        "value" : 0,
        "relation" : "eq"
      },
      "max_score" : null,
      "hits" : [ ]
  }
}
```

We are getting no restaurant within a 1 KM range, so let's increase the distance from to 2 KM and see what Elasticsearch returns. Now, we must execute the following command:

```
GET restaurants/_search
{
    "query": {
        "bool" : {
            "must" : {
                "match_all" : {}
            },
            "filter" : {
                "geo_distance" : {
                    "distance" : "2km",
                    "location" : "28.580116, 77.051673"
                }
            }
        }
    }
}
```

After executing the preceding command, we will get the following response:

```
{
  "took" : 2,
  "timed_out" : false,
  "_shards" : {
    "total" : 1,
```

```
        "successful" : 1,
        "skipped" : 0,
        "failed" : 0
    },
    "hits" : {
      "total" : {
        "value" : 3,
        "relation" : "eq"
      },
      "max_score" : 1.0,
      "hits" : [
        {
          "_index" : "restaurants",
          "_type" : "_doc",
          "_id" : "8EvB-XEBL3C-ByPYIkGW",
          "_score" : 1.0,
          "_source" : {
            "name" : "Restaurant 1",
            "location" : "28.594817, 77.046608"
          }
        },
        {
          "_index" : "restaurants",
          "_type" : "_doc",
          "_id" : "8UvE-XEBL3C-ByPYIUEs",
          "_score" : 1.0,
          "_source" : {
            "name" : "Restaurant 2",
            "location" : "28.593168, 77.041244"
          }
        },
        {
          "_index" : "restaurants",
```

```
    "_type" : "_doc",
    "_id" : "80vE-XEBL3C-ByPYkUG6",
    "_score" : 1.0,
    "_source" : {
      "name" : "Restaurant 4",
      "location" : "28.590606, 77.062959"
    }
  }
]
}
}
```

Now, we can see three restaurants within a 2 KM range: Restaurant 1, Restaurant 2, and Restaurant 4. By changing the distance, we can fetch the nearest restaurants. We can also pass the distance as a floating-point value, like 1.8km to get the restaurant within 1.8 KM range from the current location. If we search for restaurants within a 1.7 KM range, it will only return the Restaurant 4.

Aggregate restaurant based on the distance

In the other use case, we can do the aggregation to group the restaurants based on different distance ranges. We will explain aggregation in the next chapter, so don't worry if you're facing difficulty understanding aggregation here. It is required when we want to show the filter option to a user, as follows:

```
Near:               1 Restaurant
Within 2 Km:        2 Restaurants
More than 2KM away: 1 Restaurant
```

Using the preceding filter option, users can get an idea about the count of restaurants in different distance ranges. Users can then click on any option to see the restaurants within that range. We can do the aggregation based on the distance using the following query:

```
POST restaurants/_search
{
  "size": 0,
  "aggs": {
    "restaurant_in_range": {
      "geo_distance": {
```

```
      "field": "location",
      "unit": "km",
      "origin": {
        "lat": 28.580116,
        "lon": 77.051673
      },
      "ranges": [
        {
          "key": "Near",
          "from": 1,
          "to": 1.7
        },
        {
          "key": "Within 2 KM",
          "from": 1.7,
          "to": 2
        },
        {
          "key": "More than 2 KM away",
          "from": 2
        }
      ]
    }
   }
  }
 }
}
```

With this query, we can aggregate the restaurants based on their distance from the user's location ("lat": 28.580116, "lon": 77.051673). We have set the size as 0 because we only want to see the aggregation results and not the actual documents. After executing the preceding command, we will get the following response:

```
{
  "took" : 1,
  "timed_out" : false,
  "_shards" : {
```

```
    "total" : 1,
    "successful" : 1,
    "skipped" : 0,
    "failed" : 0
  },
  "hits" : {
    "total" : {
      "value" : 4,
      "relation" : "eq"
    },
    "max_score" : null,
    "hits" : [ ]
  },
  "aggregations" : {
    "restaurant_in_range" : {
      "buckets" : [
        {
          "key" : "Near",
          "from" : 1.0,
          "to" : 1.7,
          "doc_count" : 1
        },
        {
          "key" : "Within 2 KM",
          "from" : 1.7,
          "to" : 2.0,
          "doc_count" : 2
        },
        {
          "key" : "More than 2 KM away",
          "from" : 2.0,
          "doc_count" : 1
        }
```

```
        ]
      }
    }
  }
}
```

This aggregation query response shows different buckets as we have performed the bucket aggregation here. So, there are three buckets: "Near", "Within 2 KM", and "More than 2 KM away". The document count in the first bucket is 1, in the second is 2, and in the third is 1. This aggregation information is very important, as it provides the user a glimpse of the number of restaurants in different distance ranges. The user can make the decision based on this information.

Conclusion

In this chapter, we understood how to handle the geodata in Elasticsearch. We started with the geodata types, covering geo-point and geo-shape types. Under geo-point data type, we looked at how to create the mapping and save the geo-point data to the index. We also explored the different ways to represent the geodata. After geo-point, we moved on to geo-shape data and explained different shape types. Under geo-shape type, we learned how to save data in different shape types like the point, `LineString`, `Polygon`, `MultiPoint`, `MultiLineString`, `MultiPolygon`, Geometry Collection, Envelope, and Circle. After mapping and document creation, we walked through the different geo queries like `geo_distance` query, geo_polygon query, `geo_bounding_box` query, and `geo_shape` query. At the end, we covered the use cases of geo queries, where we looked at the example of restaurant data to understand the geo search and aggregation. This chapter helped you learn how to handle the geodata.

In the next chapter, we will cover data aggregation and learn different types of aggregation like metrics aggregation, bucket aggregation, pipeline aggregation, and matrix aggregation.

Questions

1. Explain the different geodata types.

2. How can we create the mapping for geo point data?

3. How can we save the geo point data?

4. What is geo shape data, and how we can create a mapping of geo shape data?

5. Explain geo queries and the different types of geo queries.

CHAPTER 9

Aggregating Your Data

Introduction

In the last chapter, we learned how to handle geodata to play with the location, like to explore things around and search things based on their coordinates. There, we explained geodata types like geo-point and geo-shape. We also looked at how to create the mapping for both types and how to add geodata in Elasticsearch. Then, we moved on to the different geo-shape types like LineString, Polygon, MultiLineString, MultiPoint, MultiPolygon, Envelope, and Circle. After adding geodata in Elasticsearch, we explored different ways to search it and explained various geo queries like `geo_distance`, `geo_polygon`, `geo_bounding_box`, and `geo_shape`. We also took a restaurant use case to explain the importance of geo queries.

In this chapter, we will see how aggregation works in Elasticsearch. Using aggregation, we can group our data and perform statistics and calculations by performing simple queries. We can analyze our whole data set using aggregation to get an overview. We can fetch the analytic view of the complete data set using aggregation.

Structure

In this chapter, we will cover the following:

- Introduction to Elasticsearch aggregation
- Bucket aggregations
- Metrics aggregations
- Pipeline aggregations
- Matrix aggregations

Objective

After studying this unit, you should be able to:

- Understand Elasticsearch aggregations
- Understand different types of aggregations like metrics, bucket, pipeline, and matrix

Introduction to Elasticsearch aggregation

Elasticsearch provides different types of aggregations based on the use case. In Elasticsearch, we can group aggregation in four major categories:

- **Bucket aggregation:** In bucket aggregation, Elasticsearch builds the buckets based on the given criteria. We can associate each bucket with the key based on the document criteria. For example, if we create the buckets for the price field, they can be "less than 500", "from 500 to 1000", "from 1001 to 1500", or "more than 1500." The documents come in the bucket based on the value of their price field. This was just an example, and we can apply bucket aggregation similarly.

- **Metrics aggregation:** We can use metrics aggregation to apply metrics over a set of documents. So, we can apply metric aggregation whenever we want to see the metrics based on some fields of the document.

- **Matrix aggregation:** The matrix aggregation works on multiple fields and creates a matrix based on the values of the documents.

- **Pipeline aggregation:** The pipeline aggregation is a grouping of more than one aggregation. Here, one aggregation's output is further aggregated.

Now, let's understand the structure of the Elasticsearch aggregation so that we can construct aggregation queries. Refer to the following expression that shows the structure of the aggregation:

```
"aggregationss|aggs" {
```

```
"<name of aggregations>" : {
 "<type of aggregations>" : {
  <body of aggregations>
 }
 }
}
```

This expression shows how we can define the aggregation. This is a very simple way to understand the Elasticsearch aggregations' structure. Now, let's understand what each line in the preceding example means:

- The fir st line shows the starting point of the aggregation query. Here, we can use the keyword "aggregations" or the short form "aggs".

- In the second line, we have to specify the aggregation name to identify it.

- In the third line, we have to specify the type of aggregation we are going to apply, like terms.

- At last, we have to specify the actual aggregation body.

This way, we can construct the aggregation query in Elasticsearch. Now, let's take an example of kibana_sample_data_flights, which we can freely download on the Kibana interface. The kibana_sample_data_flights index has the following structure:

```
{
    "_index" : "kibana_sample_data_flights",
    "_type" : "_doc",
    "_id" : "2Upz8HEBL3C-ByPYvtdI",
    "_score" : 1.0,
    "_source" : {
      "FlightNum" : "9HY9SWR",
      "DestCountry" : "AU",
      "OriginWeather" : "Sunny",
      "OriginCityName" : "Frankfurt am Main",
      "AvgTicketPrice" : 841.2656419677076,
      "DistanceMiles" : 10247.856675613455,
      "FlightDelay" : false,
      "DestWeather" : "Rain",
      "Dest" : "Sydney Kingsford Smith International Airport",
```

```
          "FlightDelayType" : "No Delay",
          "OriginCountry" : "DE",
          "dayOfWeek" : 0,
          "DistanceKilometers" : 16492.32665375846,
          "timestamp" : "2020-04-27T00:00:00",
          "DestLocation" : {
            "lat" : "-33.94609833",
            "lon" : "151.177002"
          },
          "DestAirportID" : "SYD",
          "Carrier" : "Kibana Airlines",
          "Cancelled" : false,
          "FlightTimeMin" : 1030.7704158599038,
          "Origin" : "Frankfurt am Main Airport",
          "OriginLocation" : {
            "lat" : "50.033333",
            "lon" : "8.570556"
          },
          "DestRegion" : "SE-BD",
          "OriginAirportID" : "FRA",
          "OriginRegion" : "DE-HE",
          "DestCityName" : "Sydney",
          "FlightTimeHour" : 17.179506930998397,
          "FlightDelayMin" : 0
        }
    }
```

If we want to use the preceding flight data to know aggregate using the destination country denoted with the DestCountry field, we can use the following expression:

```
GET kibana_sample_data_flights/_search
{
  "size": 0,
  "aggs": {
    "dest_country_aggregate": {
```

```
      "terms": {
        "field": "DestCountry",
        "size": 5
      }
    }
  }
}
```

We will get the following aggregation output:

```
"aggregations" : {
    "dest_country_aggregate" : {
      "doc_count_error_upper_bound" : 0,
      "sum_other_doc_count" : 5887,
      "buckets" : [
        {
          "key" : "IT",
          "doc_count" : 2371
        },
        {
          "key" : "US",
          "doc_count" : 1987
        },
        {
          "key" : "CN",
          "doc_count" : 1096
        },
        {
          "key" : "CA",
          "doc_count" : 944
        },
        {
          "key" : "JP",
          "doc_count" : 774
        }
```

```
        ]
    }
  }
```

This way, we can perform data aggregation on any index using any field. Don't worry if you are facing difficulty understanding the difference and how these aggregations work, as we will elaborate on them and provide practical examples to understand the concept and enable you to run these aggregations on your own data set. Let's start with bucket aggregation.

Bucket aggregation

We have already introduced bucket aggregation. It creates buckets, and hence the name. We can specify the field, and it will create the buckets using its unique values. We can also specify the ranges with which we want to build our custom bucket. We can use these aggregated bucket results to show the filters where a user can get the snapshot of the complete data set. For example, using the price range, a user can get an idea of how many products are there, whether there is a price bucket, or if anyone wants to know the country-wise count of any disease. Bucket aggregation can be of different types; let's start by understanding these.

Range aggregation

The range aggregation enables users to define the range, based on which the buckets are created. So, Elasticsearch uses the range condition and creates the bucket with the count of the documents matching the bucket criteria. We can provide the 'to' and 'from' values to define the bucket range. We will use the same `userdetails` index data that we referred to earlier, in *Chapter 7, Apply Search on Your Data*:

```
{
        "_index" : "userdetails",
        "_type" : "_doc",
        "_id" : "9Et3CnIBL3C-ByPYDkF8",
        "_score" : 1.0,
        "_source" : {
          "name" : "Suresh",
          "gender" : "male",
          "city" : "Singapore",
          "age" : 32
    }
}
```

Now, let's use the preceding index data to create range aggregations. We will now try to see the users in different age groups using the range aggregation. Here's an example to understand how range aggregation works:

```
GET userdetails/_search
{
  "size": 0,
  "aggs": {
    "age_range": {
      "range": {
        "field": "age",
        "ranges": [
          {
            "key": "Age range 10-20 years",
            "from": 10,
            "to": 20
          },
          {
            "key": "Age range 20-30 years",
            "from": 20,
            "to": 30
          },
          {
            "key": "Age range 30-40 years",
            "from": 30,
            "to": 40
          },
          {
            "key": "More than 40 years",
            "from": 40
          }
        ]
      }
    }
  }
}
```

```
    }
}
```

In the preceding query, we are trying to create the buckets based on the age range. We have also specified the key for each age range to make the aggregation more meaningful, as this key can help us understand the query output. We will get the following response after executing the preceding query:

```
{
  "took" : 0,
  "timed_out" : false,
  "_shards" : {
    "total" : 1,
    "successful" : 1,
    "skipped" : 0,
    "failed" : 0
  },
  "hits" : {
    "total" : {
      "value" : 6,
      "relation" : "eq"
    },
    "max_score" : null,
    "hits" : [ ]
  },
  "aggregations" : {
    "age_range" : {
      "buckets" : [
        {
          "key" : "Age range 10-20 years",
          "from" : 10.0,
          "to" : 20.0,
          "doc_count" : 1
        },
        {
          "key" : "Age range 20-30 years",
```

```
      "from" : 20.0,
      "to" : 30.0,
      "doc_count" : 1
    },
    {
      "key" : "Age range 30-40 years",
      "from" : 30.0,
      "to" : 40.0,
      "doc_count" : 2
    },
    {
      "key" : "More than 40 years",
      "from" : 40.0,
      "doc_count" : 2
    }
  ]
 }
 }
}
```

This response shows the range aggregation on the age field of the `userdetails` index. In the aggregation result, we can see different buckets with the key value and the total number of documents under the `doc_count` field. This way, we can perform range aggregation on any numeric field.

Composite aggregation

We can use composite aggregation to create a composite bucket that holds a combination of the values. Using composite aggregation, we can easily create paginated results for a large aggregation result set. We pass the source parameter to the composite aggregation, and this parameter controls the sources with which the composite bucket is built. There are three types of sources for the composite aggregations:

Terms

The terms value source is similar to the terms aggregation that we will cover soon. In this type, the values for a given field are extracted for constructing the buckets. Each bucket shows the unique field value, along with the number of documents having that field value. The following example shows composite aggregation with source value as terms:

```
GET userdetails/_search
{
  "size": 1,
  "aggs": {
    "age_range": {
      "composite": {
        "sources": [
          {
            "age": {
              "terms": {
                "field": "age"
              }
            }
          }
        ]
      }
    }
  }
}
```

We will get the following response:

```
"aggregations": {
    "age_range": {
        "after_key": {
            "age": 52
        },
        "buckets": [{
                "key": {
                    "age": 15
                },
                "doc_count": 1
            },
```

```
            {
                    "key": {
                            "age": 20
                    },
                    "doc_count": 1
            },
            {
                    "key": {
                            "age": 32
                    },
                    "doc_count": 1
            },
            {
                    "key": {
                            "age": 37
                    },
                    "doc_count": 1
            },
            {
                    "key": {
                            "age": 42
                    },
                    "doc_count": 1
            },
            {
                    "key": {
                            "age": 52
                    },
                    "doc_count": 1
            }
        ]
    }
}
```

In the preceding result, we can see the bucket with the key as the age and the count of documents under the doc_count field.

Histogram

Composite aggregation uses the histogram value source to build buckets with fixed size intervals using numeric values. We can pass the interval parameter to define the way numeric field value will transform into a histogram. Refer to this example where we have set the age interval to 10:

```
GET userdetails/_search
{
  "size": 0,
  "aggs": {
    "age_range": {
      "composite": {
        "sources": [
          {
            "age_histo": {
              "histogram": {
                "field": "age"
                , "interval": 10
              }
            }
          }
        ]
      }
    }
  }
}
```

We will get the following response:

```
  "aggregations" : {
    "age_range" : {
      "after_key" : {
        "age_histo" : 50.0
      },
```

```
    "buckets" : [
      {
        "key" : {
          "age_histo" : 10.0
        },
        "doc_count" : 1
      },
      {
        "key" : {
          "age_histo" : 20.0
        },
        "doc_count" : 1
      },
      {
        "key" : {
          "age_histo" : 30.0
        },
        "doc_count" : 2
      },
      {
        "key" : {
          "age_histo" : 40.0
        },
        "doc_count" : 1
      },
      {
        "key" : {
          "age_histo" : 50.0
        },
        "doc_count" : 1
      }
    ]
  }
}
```

This way, we can perform composite aggregation using the histogram as source value.

Date histogram

The date histogram is similar to the histogram, except we use the date/time expression for the interval parameter in the date histogram. So we can opt for the date histogram instead of the histogram source value for composite aggregation whenever we want to use the date-time for setting the interval instead of the numeric interval.

Terms aggregation

Using terms aggregation, Elasticsearch can create dynamic buckets based on the unique values for that field. This aggregation is very important to get an overview of a field value, like how the values are distributed among different documents or which value is most prominent and which one is the least prominent. We can use the terms aggregation to fetch these types of details. The following expression provides an example of terms aggregation:

```
GET userdetails/_search
{
  "size": 0,
  "aggs": {
    "age_terms_aggregation": {
      "terms": {
        "field": "age",
        "size": 10
      }
    }
  }
}
```

We can use the preceding expression to apply the terms aggregation on the age field of the userdetails index. After executing the preceding command, we will get the following response from Elasticsearch:

```
"aggregations" : {
  "age_terms_aggregation" : {
    "doc_count_error_upper_bound" : 0,
```

```
    "sum_other_doc_count" : 0,
    "buckets" : [
      {
        "key" : 20,
        "doc_count" : 2
      },
      {
        "key" : 32,
        "doc_count" : 2
      },
      {
        "key" : 15,
        "doc_count" : 1
      },
      {
        "key" : 42,
        "doc_count" : 1
      },
      {
        "key" : 52,
        "doc_count" : 1
      }
    ]
  }
}
```

The response shows that there are five age values available in the userdetails index: 15, 20, 32, 42, and 52. Each age value is shown as a bucket, where we can see the total number of documents through the doc_count field. In response, we can see some keys like doc_count_error_upper_bound and sum_other_doc_count before the bucket key. The value of the doc_count_error_upper_bound key shows the upper bound of the error, which can occur during document count for each aggregated field value. The value of the sum_other_doc_count key is the sum of all document counts among all buckets. If the bucket count is too large because of too many unique values, Elasticsearch only shows the top terms, and we can refer to the `sum_other_doc_count` value to know the complete document count in such cases. This way, we can apply the terms aggregation on any field.

Filter aggregation

Using filter aggregation, we can aggregate the data in a single bucket by applying a filter on the data. We can use this aggregation to narrow down the aggregation to certain filter conditions instead of a complete set of data. Let's take an example of the same `userdetails` index data. Now, how can we determine the average age of all males in the data? The answer is to use the filter aggregation, as it is well suited for this aggregation. The following expression explains how the filter aggregation works:

```
GET userdetails/_search
{
  "size": 0,
  "aggs": {
    "age_filter": {
      "filter": {
        "term": {
          "gender": "male"
        }
      },
      "aggs": {
        "avg_age_male": {
          "avg": {
            "field": "age"
          }
        }
      }
    }
  }
}
```

Here, we are first applying the filter to select the only male by providing the condition for gender as male. After that, we are applying the actual aggregation to find the average age. Refer to the following result received after executing the preceding command:

```
"aggregations" : {
    "age_filter" : {
        "doc_count" : 5,
        "avg_age_male" : {
            "value" : 35.6
        }
    }
}
```

This Elasticsearch response shows a single bucket where we can see the `avg_age_male` key, which we have applied in the query. The value against the key is 35.6, which means the average age of males in this data set is 35.6. This way, we can use the filter aggregation when we need to apply a filter before the actual aggregation.

Filters aggregation

Using filters aggregation, we can create a multi bucket aggregation where each bucket is created with a filter. We can think of it as aggregating an index with multiple filters to create multiple buckets. The following expression provides an example of filters aggregation:

```
GET userdetails/_search
{
  "size": 0,
  "aggs" : {
    "messages" : {
      "filters": {
        "filters" : {
          "male" :    { "term" : { "gender" : "male"    }},
          "female" : { "term" : { "gender" : "female" }}
        }
      }
    }
  }
}
```

Here, we are applying the filters aggregation using the gender field of the `userdetails` index. We are trying to create two buckets: one for the male and the other for the female gender:

```
"aggregations" : {
    "messages" : {
        "buckets" : {
            "female" : {
                "doc_count" : 2
            },
            "male" : {
                "doc_count" : 5
            }
        }
    }
}
```

This response shows two buckets, wherein the female bucket is shows `doc_count` as 2, and the male bucket shows `doc_count` as 5. Similarly, we can apply the filters aggregation on any field where we want to create more than one bucket.

Geo distance aggregation

We discussed geo data in the last chapter, and the geo distance bucket aggregation supports the aggregation of geodata. Using this aggregation, we can aggregate the documents with distance from a central point. For example, if we want to know the count of documents that ranges from a certain distance to a coordinate. We will take the same restaurant example as in the last chapter. The following example explains how we can apply the geo distance aggregation:

```
POST restaurants/_search
{
    "size": 0,
    "aggs": {
        "restaurant_in_range": {
            "geo_distance": {
                "field": "location",
                "unit": "km",
```

```
        "origin": {
          "lat": 28.580116,
          "lon": 77.051673
        },
        "ranges": [
          {
            "key": "Near",
            "from": 1,
            "to": 1.7
          },
          {
            "key": "Within 2 KM",
            "from": 1.7,
            "to": 2
          },
          {
            "key": "More than 2 KM away",
            "from": 2
          }
        ]
      }
    }
  }
}
```

In the preceding example, we are fetching the restaurant documents using the distance range from a coordinate ("lat": 28.580116,"lon": 77.051673). Here, we are trying to know how many restaurants are there within 2 KM and more than 2 KM away. We will get the following output after executing the preceding command:

```
"aggregations" : {
  "available_restaurants" : {
    "buckets" : [
      {
        "key" : "Within 2 KM range",
        "from" : 1.0,
```

```
      "to" : 2.0,
      "doc_count" : 3
    },
    {
      "key" : "More than 2 KM away",
      "from" : 2.0,
      "doc_count" : 1
    }
  ]
 }
}
```

In this response, we can see that there are two buckets. In the first bucket, we can see the `doc_count` as 3, which shows the documents within the range of 2 KM. The other bucket shows 1 document count, which is more than 2 KM away from the given coordinates. This way, we can apply the distance base aggregation to know more about places situated at different distance ranges from a central point. We are not discussing several other bucket type aggregations here. We have covered some important ones, so let's move to the next type of the aggregation—metric aggregation.

Metrics aggregation

In metrics aggregation, Elasticsearch applies metrics like `sum,` `avg` and `stats` on field values after aggregating the documents. The metrics aggregation can be a single-value numeric aggregation or a multi-value numeric aggregation. The single-value numeric aggregation returns a single metrics, and an example of aggregation that comes under this type is `avg`, `max`, and `min`. The multi-value numeric aggregation returns multiple metrics like stats. Now, let's discuss some of the metrics aggregation types with examples for better understanding.

Min aggregation

The min aggregation is a single-value metrics aggregation that returns the minimum value from a numeric field after aggregating the documents. The value can be the numeric field value of the document, or it can be provided by executing the script. The following example shows min aggregation using the same `userdetails` index:

```
GET userdetails/_search
{
```

```
"size": 0,
"aggs": {
  "min_age": {
    "min": {
      "field": "age"
    }
  }
}
}
```

Here, we are fetching the minimum age from the age field value of the userdetails index. We will get the following response after executing this command:

```
"aggregations" : {
  "min_age" : {
    "value" : 15.0
  }
}
```

Here, we can see that the minimum age is 15 years, which is derived using the min aggregation. This way, we can use the min aggregation of metrics type to fetch the minimum numeric value of a field from an index in Elasticsearch.

Max aggregation

The max aggregation is a single-value metrics aggregation that returns the maximum value from a numeric field after aggregating the documents. The value can be the numeric field value of the document, or it can be provided by executing the script. This example shows max aggregation using the same userdetails index:

```
GET userdetails/_search
{
  "size": 0,
  "aggs": {
    "max_age": {
      "max": {
        "field": "age"
      }
    }
```

```
  }
}
```

Here, we are fetching the maximum age from the age field value of the `userdetails` index. Executing the preceding command will get us the following response:

```
"aggregations" : {
  "max_age" : {
    "value" : 52.0
  }
}
```

We can see that the maximum age is 52 years, which is derived using the max aggregation. This way, we can use the max aggregation of metrics type to fetch the maximum numeric value of a field from an index in Elasticsearch.

Avg aggregation

The avg aggregation is a single-value metrics aggregation that returns the average value from a numeric field after aggregating the documents. The value can be the numeric field value of the document, or it can be provided by executing the script. I can use the avg aggregation to determine the average age of user from the `userdetails` index. The following example shows avg aggregation using the same `userdetails` index:

```
GET userdetails/_search
{
  "size": 0,
  "aggs": {
    "avg_age": {
      "avg": {
        "field": "age"
      }
    }
  }
}
```

Here, we are fetching the average age from the age field value of the `userdetails` index. Executing this command will get us the following response:

```
"aggregations" : {
```

```
      "avg_age" : {
        "value" : 30.428571428571427
      }
    }
```

Here, we can see that the average age is 30.42 years, which is derived using the avg aggregation. This way, we can use the avg aggregation of metrics type to fetch the average of a numeric field from an index in Elasticsearch.

Sum aggregation

The sum aggregation is a single-value metrics aggregation that returns the sum of all numeric values from a numeric field after aggregating the documents. The value can be the numeric field value of the document, or it can be provided by executing the script. I can use the sum aggregation to know the sum of all ages of users from the userdetails index. Although the age sum is not a good example, we can use it to understand the concept. The following example shows avg aggregation using the same userdetails index:

```
GET userdetails/_search
{
  "size": 0,
  "aggs": {
    "sum_age": {
      "sum": {
        "field": "age"
      }
    }
  }
}
```

Here, we are fetching the sum of all ages from the age field value of the userdetails index. The preceding command gets us the following response:

```
  "aggregations" : {
    "sum_age" : {
      "value" : 213.0
    }
  }
```

Here, we can see that the sum of all ages is 213 years, which is derived using the sum aggregation. This way, we can use the sum aggregation of metrics type to fetch the sum metrics of a numeric field from an index in Elasticsearch.

Value count aggregation

The value count aggregation is a single-value metrics aggregation to find the count of the number of values fetched from the aggregated documents. For example, we can get the average value for the numeric field in avg aggregation, but we can use the value count aggregation if we want to know the count of the field values used to extract the average. The next example shows avg aggregation using the same `userdetails` index:

```
GET userdetails/_search
{
  "size": 0,
  "aggs": {
    "total_age_fields_count": {
      "value_count": {
        "field": "age"
      }
    }
  }
}
```

Here, we are fetching the count of age fields from the `userdetails` index. After executing the preceding command, we will get the following response:

```
"aggregations" : {
  "total_age_fields_count" : {
    "value" : 7
  }
}
```

We can see that the value count of the age field is 7, which is derived using the value count aggregation. This way, we can fetch the occurrence of a numeric field from an index in Elasticsearch using the value count aggregation of metrics type.

Stats aggregation

The stats aggregation is a multi-value metric aggregation that computes the stats of a numeric field value by aggregating the documents. These stats can be min, max, sum, count, avg, and such. The value can be the numeric field value of the document, or it can be provided by executing the script. Here's an example showing stats aggregation using the same `userdetails` index:

```
GET userdetails/_search
{
  "size": 0,
  "aggs": {
    "age_stats": {
      "stats": {
        "field": "age"
      }
    }
  }
}
```

Here, we are fetching the stats of the age fields from the `userdetails` index. After executing it, we get the following response:

```
"aggregations" : {
    "age_stats" : {
       "count" : 7,
       "min" : 15.0,
       "max" : 52.0,
       "avg" : 30.428571428571427,
       "sum" : 213.0
    }
}
```

In this response, we can see that the stats aggregation of the age field shows different details in a single aggregation, like it is showing the count as 7, min as 15, max as 52, avg as 30.48, and sum as 213. So, we can see that a single stats aggregation shows all these details for a single numeric field age derived using the stats aggregation. This way, we can use the stats aggregation of metrics type to fetch the stats of a numeric field from an index in Elasticsearch.

Extended stats aggregation

The extended stats aggregation is a multi-value metric aggregation that computes the stats of a numeric field value by aggregating the documents. The extended stats aggregation is an extended version of the stats aggregation that also displays additional details like `sum_of_square`, variance, `std_deviation`, and `std_ deviation_bounds`. The value can be the numeric field value of the document, or it can be provided by executing the script. Take a look at this example showing extended stats aggregation using the same `userdetails` index:

```
GET userdetails/_search
{
  "size": 0,
  "aggs": {
    "age_extended_stats": {
      "extended_stats": {
        "field": "age"
      }
    }
  }
}
```

Here, we are fetching the extended stats of the age fields from the `userdetails` index. After executing this command, we get the following response:

```
"aggregations" : {
  "age_extended_stats" : {
    "count" : 7,
    "min" : 15.0,
    "max" : 52.0,
    "avg" : 30.428571428571427,
    "sum" : 213.0,
    "sum_of_squares" : 7541.0,
    "variance" : 151.38775510204076,
    "std_deviation" : 12.303973142933984,
    "std_deviation_bounds" : {
      "upper" : 55.0365177144394,
      "lower" : 5.820625142703459
    }
  }
}
```

We can see that the extended stats aggregation of the age field is showing different details in a single response. It is showing the count as 7, min as 15, max as 52, avg as 30.48, sum as 213, sum_of_squares as 7541, variance as 151.38, std_deviation as 12.30, and std_deviation_bounds where the upper is 55.03 and lower is 5.8. So, we can see that a single extended stats aggregation shows all these details for a single numeric field age derived using the extended stats aggregation. This way, we can use the extended stats aggregation of metrics type to fetch the extended stats of a numeric field from an index in Elasticsearch.

Percentiles aggregation

The percentiles aggregation is a multi-value metric aggregation that calculates one or more percentiles over a numeric field value by aggregating the documents. The value can be the numeric field value of the document, or it can be provided by executing the script. The following example shows percentiles aggregation using the same userdetails index:

```
GET userdetails/_search
{
  "size": 0,
  "aggs": {
    "age_percentile": {
      "percentiles": {
        "field": "age"
      }
    }
  }
}
```

Here, we are fetching the percentiles of the age fields from the userdetails index. The default percentiles of the percentiles aggregation are 1, 5, 25, 50, 75, 95, 99. After executing the preceding command, we get the following response:

```
"aggregations" : {
  "age_extended_stats" : {
    "values" : {
      "1.0" : 15.0,
      "5.0" : 15.0,
      "25.0" : 20.0,
```

```
        "50.0" : 32.0,
        "75.0" : 39.5,
        "95.0" : 52.0,
        "99.0" : 52.0
      }
    }
  }
```

In this response, we can see different percentiles and the calculated values against these percentiles. This way, we can use the percentiles aggregation of metrics type to fetch different percentiles of a numeric field from an index in Elasticsearch.

Matrix aggregation

The matrix aggregation works on multiple fields of the index and creates a matrix using the extracted values from the given fields of the document. The matrix aggregation does not support scripts.

Matrix stats aggregation

The matrix stats aggregation is a matrix aggregation that works on single or multiple numeric fields and computes the statistics like count, mean, variance, skewness, kurtosis, covariance, correlation, and such. We can apply it on more than one numeric field, but we will use it on the age field using the same userdetails index example. This example shows matrix stats aggregation using the same userdetails index:

```
GET userdetails/_search
{
  "size": 0,
  "aggs": {
    "age_matrix_stats": {
      "matrix_stats": {
        "fields": ["age"]
      }
    }
  }
}
```

In this example, we are fetching the matrix stats of the age fields from the userdetails index. After executing this command, we get the following response:

```
"aggregations" : {
  "age_matrix_stats" : {
    "doc_count" : 7,
    "fields" : [
      {
        "name" : "age",
        "count" : 7,
        "mean" : 30.428571428571434,
        "variance" : 176.61904761904768,
        "skewness" : 0.4336291862091775,
        "kurtosis" : 1.9621816119745739,
        "covariance" : {
          "age" : 176.61904761904768
        },
        "correlation" : {
          "age" : 1.0
        }
      }
    ]
  }
}
```

We can see different stats for the age field. This way, we can use the matrix stats aggregation to fetch different stats like mean, variance, skewness, kurtosis, covariance, and correlation of a numeric field from an index in Elasticsearch.

Pipeline aggregation

The pipeline aggregation is a type of aggregation that does not work on document sets and uses the output from other aggregations. There are mainly two families of pipeline aggregations: parent and sibling. This aggregation saves the additional document scan for fetching the aggregation results; instead, it uses the sibling aggregation output for the input. Pipeline aggregation can have two sections:

- **Parent:** Parent is a family of pipeline aggregation where the aggregation is performed on the output of a parent aggregation. In the parent family, the pipeline aggregation can compute new buckets or apply new aggregations to the existing buckets.

- **Sibling:** Sibling is a family of pipeline aggregation where the aggregation is performed on the output of a sibling aggregation. Here, the pipeline aggregations work on the same level as the sibling aggregation.

Now, let's cover the different types of pipeline aggregation in detail and look at practical examples to understand them better.

Avg bucket aggregation

The avg bucket aggregation is a pipeline aggregation of the sibling families. It calculates the average value of the output of the sibling aggregation, which must be a multi-bucket aggregation. The following example illustrates the average bucket aggregation using the same `userdetails` index:

```
GET userdetails/_search
{
  "size": 0,
  "aggs": {
    "age_range": {
      "range": {
        "field": "age",
        "ranges": [
          {
            "key": "Age range 10-20 years",
            "from": 10,
            "to": 20
          },
          {
            "key": "Age range 20-30 years",
            "from": 20,
            "to": 30
          },
          {
            "key": "Age range 30-40 years",
            "from": 30,
            "to": 40
          },
          {
```

```
          "key": "More than 40 years",
          "from": 40
        }
      ]
    },
    "aggs": {
      "avg_age": {
        "avg": {
          "field": "age"
        }
      }
    }
  },
  "total_avg_age": {
    "avg_bucket": {
      "buckets_path": "age_range>avg_age"
    }
  }
  }
}
```

Here, we are fetching the average age value in each bucket. Now, we are creating the additional aggregation to fetch the total avg age for the userdetails index using this bucket. Executing the preceding command will get us the following response:

```
"aggregations" : {
  "age_range" : {
    "buckets" : [
      {
        "key" : "Age range 10-20 years",
        "from" : 10.0,
        "to" : 20.0,
        "doc_count" : 1,
        "avg_age" : {
          "value" : 15.0
        }
      },
```

```
        {
          "key" : "Age range 20-30 years",
          "from" : 20.0,
          "to" : 30.0,
          "doc_count" : 2,
          "avg_age" : {
            "value" : 20.0
          }
        },
        {
          "key" : "Age range 30-40 years",
          "from" : 30.0,
          "to" : 40.0,
          "doc_count" : 2,
          "avg_age" : {
            "value" : 32.0
          }
        },
        {
          "key" : "More than 40 years",
          "from" : 40.0,
          "doc_count" : 2,
          "avg_age" : {
            "value" : 47.0
          }
        }
      ]
    },
    "total_avg_age" : {
      "value" : 28.5
    }
  }
```

Here, we can see that each bucket has an `avg_age` field inside, along with the `doc_count`, which is showing the average age for that bucket. We have applied the additional aggregation to get the total avg age, which is using the preceding sibling bucket aggregation as an input for calculating the total avg age. This way, we can use the average bucket aggregation of pipeline type to apply additional aggregation on a sibling aggregation to get the desired results in Elasticsearch.

Max bucket aggregation

The max bucket aggregation is similar to the avg bucket aggregation, the only difference being max bucket aggregation is used to fetch the max value instead of the average. The following example shows the average bucket aggregation using the same userdetails index:

```
GET userdetails/_search
{
  "size": 0,
  "aggs": {
    "age_range": {
      "range": {
        "field": "age",
        "ranges": [
          {
            "key": "Age range 10-30 years",
            "from": 10,
            "to": 30
          },
          {
            "key": "More than 30 years",
            "from": 30
          }
        ]
      },
      "aggs": {
        "avg_age": {
          "avg": {
            "field": "age"
          }
        }
      }
    }
```

```
    },
    "total_max_age": {
      "max_bucket": {
        "buckets_path": "age_range>avg_age"
      }
    }
  }
}
```

Here, we are fetching the max age value in each bucket. We are now using this bucket to create the additional aggregation to fetch the overall max age for the **userdetails** index. This aggregation saves the additional document scan for fetching the aggregation results; instead, it uses the sibling aggregation output for the input. Executing the preceding command gets us the following response:

```
"aggregations" : {
  "age_range" : {
    "buckets" : [
      {
        "key" : "Age range 10-30 years",
        "from" : 10.0,
        "to" : 30.0,
        "doc_count" : 3,
        "avg_age" : {
          "value" : 18.333333333333332
        }
      },
      {
        "key" : "More than 30 years",
        "from" : 30.0,
        "doc_count" : 4,
        "avg_age" : {
          "value" : 39.5
        }
      }
    ]
  },
```

```
  "total_max_age" : {
    "value" : 39.5,
    "keys" : [
      "More than 30 years"
    ]
  }
}
```

Here, we can see that each bucket has an `avg_age` field inside, along with the `doc_count`, which shows the average age for that bucket. We have applied the additional aggregation to get the overall max age, which is using the preceding sibling bucket aggregation as an input to calculate the max age. This way, we can use the max bucket aggregation of pipeline type to apply additional aggregation on a sibling aggregation to get the desired results in Elasticsearch. Similarly, we have min bucket aggregation where we fetch the min value instead of the max value using the `min_bucket` option.

Sum bucket aggregation

The sum bucket aggregation is a pipeline aggregation of the sibling families. It calculates the sum of the specified field from all buckets of the sibling aggregation. This example illustrates the average bucket aggregation using the same `userdetails` index:

```
GET userdetails/_search
{
  "size": 0,
  "aggs": {
    "age_range": {
      "range": {
        "field": "age",
        "ranges": [
          {
            "key": "Age range 10-30 years",
            "from": 10,
            "to": 30
          },
          {
            "key": "More than 30 years",
```

```
        "from": 30
      }
    ]
  },
  "aggs": {
    "avg_age": {
      "avg": {
        "field": "age"
      }
    }
  }
},
"total_sum_age": {
  "sum_bucket": {
    "buckets_path": "age_range>avg_age"
  }
}
}
}
}
```

Here, we are calculating the sum of the **avg_age** field from each bucket. We will get the following response after executing the preceding command:

```
"aggregations" : {
  "age_range" : {
    "buckets" : [
      {
        "key" : "Age range 10-30 years",
        "from" : 10.0,
        "to" : 30.0,
        "doc_count" : 3,
        "avg_age" : {
          "value" : 18.333333333333332
        }
      },
      {
```

```
          "key" : "More than 30 years",
          "from" : 30.0,
          "doc_count" : 4,
          "avg_age" : {
            "value" : 39.5
          }
        }
      ]
    },
    "total_sum_age" : {
      "value" : 57.83333333333333
    }
  }
}
```

In the preceding response, we can see that each bucket has a `avg_age` field, along with the `doc_count` inside, which shows the average age for that bucket. We have applied the additional aggregation to get the sum of the `avg_age` field from all buckets.

Conclusion

In this chapter, we covered Elasticsearch aggregation and learned how to aggregate data. We started with an introduction to aggregation and understood what aggregation is and why we need it. Then, we explored different types of aggregations, like bucket aggregation, metrics aggregation, matrix aggregation, and pipeline aggregation. We also looked at practical examples for better understanding. This chapter would have taught you how to perform data aggregation using Elasticsearch aggregation.

The next chapter will walk you through improving the Elasticsearch performance. We will learn how to tune the Elasticsearch indexing speed, search speed, and disk usage, and we will also cover the best practices for Elasticsearch.

Questions

1. What is Elasticsearch aggregation?
2. Explain the different types of aggregations.
3. Give an example of the range aggregation.
4. What is geo distance aggregation?
5. What is matrix aggregation?

CHAPTER 10
Improving the Performance

Introduction

In the last chapter, we covered Elasticsearch aggregation, where we understood how to aggregate data. We also learned what aggregation is and why we need it. We looked at different types of aggregations like bucket aggregation, metrics aggregation, matrix aggregation, and pipeline aggregation. In this chapter, we will look at how to improve Elasticsearch performance. We will also see how to tune the Elasticsearch indexing speed, search speed, and disk usage. At the end of the chapter, we will explain the best practices for Elasticsearch.

Structure

In this chapter, we will cover the following:

- Tuning Elasticsearch indexing speed
- Tuning Elasticsearch search speed
- Tuning Elasticsearch for disk usage
- Elasticsearch best practices

Objectives

After studying this unit, you should be able to:

- Tune Elasticsearch performance
- Understand the best practices

Introduction

Elasticsearch is fast when we talk about indexing, searching, and aggregating data, but this is not the case every time. When the data size increases, we can see its effects on the performance; also, it depends on different use cases. In some cases, the application can be index intensive, while other applications can search intensively. So, there is no balance and ideal use case, which is why we have to work on certain trade-off as per the use case. In this chapter, we will discuss different ways to tune the Elasticsearch indexing speed, search speed, disk usage utilization, and best practices.

We cannot optimize all use cases like indexing, searching, aggregation, so we must understand the business priorities and do some trade-off for less important things. So, these trade-offs can be decided based on the more important things. We also need to do some benchmarking to understand how optimization is performing and whether it is improving overall performance. Instead of completing all tuning, it is better to do one at a time and check the impact before moving any further. Now, if our application is more index intensive, we can apply less search and more data indexing, so we can follow the options to tune indexing speed. If the application is search intensive, we can use the options to tune the search speed. Now, let's discuss how we can tune the Elasticsearch indexing speed.

Tuning Elasticsearch indexing speed

Let's see the option we can perform to optimize the indexing speed. You need to understand whether your application is search intensive or index intensive and take the optimization decisions accordingly. Sometimes, it is required to push a lot of data at once, like if we are migrating data from any source to Elasticsearch. We can optimize the index performance for a shorter period for such situations, and we can revert the changes once the migration is complete. So, we can tweak the Elasticsearch cluster performance as per the application use case demand. Now, let's discuss some options to optimize the Elasticsearch indexing performance.

Bulk requests instead of a single request

We can improve the indexing performance using bulk requests instead of a single-document index request, but how much data we can send in a single request is a question, as this number can be extracted only through benchmarking. For example, if we have a lot of documents to index, we can start with 100-200 documents and gradually increase it unless we get a performance issue. This way, we can get the optimal number of documents that can be indexed in bulk based on the Elasticsearch cluster we are using. If we add too many documents for a single index request, it will create memory pressure on the Elasticsearch cluster. We must execute the following command for a bulk indexing request:

```
POST _bulk
{ "index" : { "_index" : "users", "_id" : "1" } }
{ "name" : "Anurag Srivastava" }
{ "index" : { "_index" : "users", "_id" : "2" } }
{ "name" : "Rakesh Kumar" }
{ "create" : { "_index" : "users", "_id" : "3" } }
{ "name" : "Vinod Kambli" }
{ "update" : {"_id" : "2", "_index" : "users"} }
{ "doc" : { "name" : "Suresh Raina" }}
```

Here, we are performing multiple operations in a single bulk request. We are creating the documents with id 1, 2, and 3 and updating the document with id 2. We can also delete a document using the bulk request. After executing the preceding request, we will get the following response:

```
{
  "took" : 384,
  "errors" : false,
  "items" : [
    {
      "index" : {
        "_index" : "users",
        "_type" : "_doc",
        "_id" : "1",
        "_version" : 1,
        "result" : "created",
        "_shards" : {
          "total" : 2,
          "successful" : 1,
          "failed" : 0
```

```
      },
      "_seq_no" : 0,
      "_primary_term" : 1,
      "status" : 201
    }
  },
  {
    "index" : {
      "_index" : "users",
      "_type" : "_doc",
      "_id" : "2",
      "_version" : 1,
      "result" : "created",
      "_shards" : {
        "total" : 2,
        "successful" : 1,
        "failed" : 0
      },
      "_seq_no" : 1,
      "_primary_term" : 1,
      "status" : 201
    }
  },
  {
    "create" : {
      "_index" : "users",
      "_type" : "_doc",
      "_id" : "3",
      "_version" : 1,
      "result" : "created",
      "_shards" : {
        "total" : 2,
        "successful" : 1,
```

```
          "failed" : 0
        },
        "_seq_no" : 2,
        "_primary_term" : 1,
        "status" : 201
      }
    },
    {
      "update" : {
        "_index" : "users",
        "_type" : "_doc",
        "_id" : "2",
        "_version" : 2,
        "result" : "updated",
        "_shards" : {
          "total" : 2,
          "successful" : 1,
          "failed" : 0
        },
        "_seq_no" : 3,
        "_primary_term" : 1,
        "status" : 200
      }
    }
  ]
}
```

In this response, we can see the output for each operation we performed in the bulk request. We can see three create requests and one update request. This way, we can perform multiple index operations in a single bulk request, and we can also include create, update, and delete operations.

Smart use of the Elasticsearch Cluster

We should use the Elasticsearch cluster smartly, like if we need to make bulk requests for a huge set of data, we can use multiple threads and processes to handle the data. This way, we can complement the bulk indexing by providing the maximum capacity to handle more requests. To utilize all Elasticsearch cluster resources, we should use multiple threads or processes of Elasticsearch. The optimal number of workers or threads can only be extracted using benchmarking, as it can vary for different clusters. To benchmark the number of workers, we can gradually increase it and monitor the I/O and CPU, stopping when the cluster I/O or CPU saturates. This is another factor that we can work on to compliment the bulk upload, and these two together can provide a good performance boost for data indexing.

Increasing the refresh interval

The refresh interval is the interval after which the indexed document can be ready for the search operations. So, we wait for the next refresh for an indexed document to appear in the search operation, and this duration is defined using the Elasticsearch `refresh_interval` setting. The default value of `refresh_interval` is 1s, so every newly indexed document can be searched after a second at most. However, this 1s refresh only happens if Elasticsearch indices receive one or more search requests within the last 30 seconds. Getting back to the index performance tuning, we should increase the `refresh_interval` because this is a costly operation and can affect the indexing performance. We can define the `index.refresh_interval` setting using the Elasticsearch configuration file, or it can be achieved at each index level through index settings using the query. So, if we want to perform bulk indexing, we can increase the `refresh_interval` to a higher value, like the 30s or more. This way, we can avoid the index refresh that may occur every 1s. So, we can improve indexing performance by increasing the `refresh_inteval`.

Disable replicas

We can disable the index replication to improve indexing performance. This option is well suited when we want to load a large amount of data into Elasticsearch. We can set the `index.number_of_replicas` setting to 0 to improve indexing performance, and we can change this setting using the `elasticsearch.yml` file or the setting API. Removing the data replication causes a risk of data loss if the node fails, and we should handle this issue by saving the data at some other place as well. Once the data is written successfully, we can enable the replication using the `index.number_of_replicas` setting. By disabling the replication, we can ensure that Elasticsearch will not have to do additional work to replicate the data on other nodes. This way, it is advisable to disable the replication until the data is loaded in Elasticsearch when we want to push a large amount of data.

Using auto-generated ids

During document indexing, Elasticsearch has to make an additional effort if you use any pre-defined index id field value, which affects performance. The index id field must be unique, and Elasticsearch has to check the id in the existing document to verify this. If the id is unavailable, only the document can be indexed. If the id is already available in the same shard, Elasticsearch will throw an error. We can fix this additional work done by Elasticsearch using auto-generated ids, as it will skip the check and can enhance Elasticsearch index performance. So, we should use the auto-generated ids unless it is important to use our id value.

Tweaking the indexing buffer size

In the case of heavy indexing, the nodes use 512 MB size per shard at most. We should ensure that the `indices.memory.index_buffer_size` is large enough to make data indexing smooth for heavy indexing. In Elasticsearch, we can configure this setting as some percentage of the Java heap size or provide an absolute byte-size. By default, Elasticsearch uses 10% of the JVM memory for the index buffer size and it is plenty in many use cases. Let's say our JVM size is 10GB of memory, so the index buffer size would be 1GB, which is sufficient to host two heavy indexed shards. This way, we can decide the best size for the index buffer through benchmarking.

Use of faster hardware

To increase indexing performance, we can also use faster drives like SSD drives as their performance is better as compared to the spinning disks. We should always prefer local storage instead of a remote filesystem like SMB or NFS. Virtualized storage like AWS Elastic Block Storage should also be avoided. Cloud storage is easy to set up, and it is fast as well, but it is slower than dedicated local storage for the ongoing process, which is why local storage is better. So, we can improve indexing performance using SSD drives.

Allocating memory to the filesystem cache

We can buffer the I/O operation using the filesystem cache. This can provide a performance boost because the cache can be used as a buffer. For the filesystem cache, we can assign half of the memory on the node running Elasticsearch.

Tuning Elasticsearch search speed

We have covered some ways to tune indexing performance. Now, let's look at some ways using to optimize the search speed. We can use these options if the application is search intensive instead of index intensive. In many cases, data indexing is not frequent, but we perform an intensive search in the application. For example, in an e-commerce application, we push the product details once, after which they are searched by different users. In these situations, our main focus is to improve the search performance of the cluster. As per the application use case demand, we can tweak the Elasticsearch cluster performance. Now, we will discuss some options to optimize the Elasticsearch search performance.

Document modelling

We should do a document modelling as per the application requirement. The main focus of modelling should be to avoid joins or parent-child relationship. For example, if we want to show the product detail page, it is good to keep all required attributes in a single index so that the page can be loaded quickly. If we don't do such mapping, we might feel a slight delay to fetch data from different indices. So, document modelling is an important aspect of tuning Elasticsearch search performance.

Search a few fields if possible

If we want to improve the search performance, it's best to search as few fields as possible. The problem occurs when we add more fields to search using `query_string` or `multi_search`; it takes more time to fetch the results. It is useful if we can reduce this count, but there may be more than one field sometimes. Let's say there are two fields on which we need to apply the search. For those situations, Elasticsearch provides a way to copy the value of more than one field to a single field and we can then apply our data search using that single field. Using the copy-to directive of Elasticsearch, we can create a copy of field value to a different field. Refer to the following example with two different fields: `first_name` and `last_name`:

```
PUT user_details
{
  "mappings": {
    "properties": {
      "name": {
        "type": "text"
      },
      "first_name": {
        "type": "text",
        "copy_to": "name"
      },
      "last_first": {
        "type": "text",
        "copy_to": "name"
      }
```

```
      }
    }
}
```

Here, we are creating the mapping where we have two fields: first_name and last_name. During search, a user can type anything as the first_name or the last_name and we have to apply search on both fields for that. However, we are using the copy_to directive to copy the value of both fields to a different field, which is the name. After executing this command, we can test this by adding a document; here's an example:

```
POST user_details/_doc/
{
    "first_name" : "Anurag",
    "last_name" : "Srivastava"
}
```

Using the preceding command, we have added a single document to the user_details index, which we just created. Now, let's search the record to verify that data is copied to the new field, using which we can apply the data search. We can execute the following command to search on the new field:

```
GET user_details/_search?q=name:Anurag
```

In the preceding example, you can see that I am running a URI search where the field name is the name, but we have not provided this field for document creation. Now, let's look at the Elasticsearch response after executing the preceding command:

```
{
  "took" : 197,
  "timed_out" : false,
  "_shards" : {
    "total" : 1,
    "successful" : 1,
    "skipped" : 0,
    "failed" : 0
  },
  "hits" : {
    "total" : {
      "value" : 1,
```

```
        "relation" : "eq"
    },
    "max_score" : 0.6931471,
    "hits" : [
        {
            "_index" : "user_details",
            "_type" : "_doc",
            "_id" : "W_KNLnIBV6DMUX9AYs9b",
            "_score" : 0.6931471,
            "_source" : {
                "first_name" : "Anurag",
                "last_name" : "Srivastava"
            }
        }
    ]
    }
}
```

This way, we can use the name field to search the records, and it is quite useful when we want to put data of more than one field in a single field, using which we can reduce the field count for data search. This way, we can improve the search performance of Elasticsearch.

Pre-index data

We can use the search pattern information to optimize data indexing behavior. Here, we can use indexing to improve the search performance; for example, if we want to aggregate data to show the range bucket (like shoe size range), it costs us to aggregate the data during the search. It is better if we can put the range when we are indexing the document so that we can save the aggregation cost and enhance search performance. Let's take an example where the document structure is as follows:

```
POST index/_doc/
{
    "product category": "Formal shoes",
    "size": 7
}
```

Now, we must execute the following command to aggregate the data to know about different ranges:

```
GET index/_search
{
  "aggs": {
    "size_ranges": {
      "range": {
        "field": "size",
        "ranges": [
          {
            "to": 6
          },
          {
            "from": 6,
            "to": 12
          },
          {
            "from": 12
          }
        ]
      }
    }
  }
}
```

We will get the following aggregation output, along with the documents:

```
"aggregations" : {
  "size_ranges" : {
    "buckets" : [
      {
        "key" : "*-6.0",
        "to" : 6.0,
        "doc_count" : 0
      },
```

```
        {
          "key" : "6.0-12.0",
          "from" : 6.0,
          "to" : 12.0,
          "doc_count" : 5
        },
        {
          "key" : "12.0-*",
          "from" : 12.0,
          "doc_count" : 2
        }
      ]
    }
  }
```

We have to execute the range aggregation on the data set for the size range filter, but how about we create this range detail during index time of the document . That way, we can save the range aggregation cost as the range aggregation can directly, we applied on a single field, and we need not apply the range aggregation . Let's take an example to understand how we can add this additional detail during document indexing:

```
PUT index
{
  "mappings": {
    "properties": {
      "size_range": {
        "type": "keyword"
      }
    }
  }
}
```

In the preceding example, we are creating the mapping for the `size_range` field to add the size range along with the shoe name and size. Now, we can add some documents to the index by executing the following command:

```
POST index/_doc/
{
  "product category": "Formal shoes",
  "size": 5,
  "size_range": "0-5"
}
```

In the preceding query, we are adding the document and also the `size_range` field to store the size range of the show. We need not aggregate it using a range aggregation, but using terms aggregation can easily show different ranges by picking the unique values of the `size_range` field. We can apply the size range aggregation using the query given here:

```
GET index/_search
{
  "aggs": {
    "size_ranges": {
      "terms": {
        "field": "size_range"
      }
    }
  }
}
```

Now, we are aggregating the results using the `size_range` field. We will get the following aggregation response after executing the preceding query:

```
"aggregations" : {
    "size_ranges" : {
        "doc_count_error_upper_bound" : 0,
        "sum_other_doc_count" : 0,
        "buckets" : [
          {
            "key" : "0-5",
            "doc_count" : 1
          },
          {
```

```
        "key" : "10-15",
        "doc_count" : 1
    },
    {
        "key" : "6-10",
        "doc_count" : 1
    }
  ]
 }
}
```

This way, we can pre-index data to save the additional cost during the search. We just need to identify the fields that we can add along with the actual document data.

Mapping of identifiers as keyword

There are many numeric fields for which we may not need numeric operations to be performed, like the id field of any table like product id and blog id. So, it is not useful to define them as numeric because Elasticsearch optimizes the numeric fields for the range queries. For example, if we have a price, quantity, or size, we would like to get the range using aggregation, and we should keep these fields numeric for that. For other numeric values like blog id and product id, it is good if we can define them as keyword fields. This is because it helps perform term queries, and we mostly want to perform term queries on such fields. Also, the term queries for keyword fields are faster than the term queries on the numeric field. This way, we can tune the search performance of Elasticsearch by planning the proper data type.

We should force merge the read-only indices

It is always good to merge the read-only shards of indices into a single segment. A single segment has a simpler and efficient data structure that enables us to perform a better search. The time-based indices are the best examples where we can apply the force merge because we cannot get more new documents in the index once the current time frame is over. So, these types are indices are typically read-only, and we can apply the force merge. We should not force merge an index if it is open for writing currently or soon.

Use filter instead of the query

A query clause can be used to determine how well a document is matching, while a filter term is used to find whether a document matches a given query parameter. So,

Elasticsearch does not calculate the relevancy score for a filter clause, and the results can also be cached in case of a filter. So, we should prefer the filter instead of a query if the relevancy score is not required.

Increase the replica count

The search performance of Elasticsearch can be improved by increasing the replica count for the index. Elasticsearch uses the primary or replica shard to perform the search, and increasing the replica shards can make more nodes available for the search.

Fetch only the required fields

We can select only required fields instead of fetching all the fields of the index. Refer to the following index data for an example:

```
{
        "_index" : "index",
        "_type" : "_doc",
        "_id" : "7OssOHIBCxugYrgStg5D",
        "_score" : 1.0,
        "_source" : {
           "product category" : "Formal shoes",
           "size" : 14,
           "size_range" : "10-15"
        }
}
```

Here, we have three fields returned when we query the index. Now, we can execute the following query if we just need the product category instead of all fields:

```
GET index/_search
{
  "_source": ["product category"],
  "query" : {
        "term" : {
                          "size" : 14
                          }
              }
}
```

We will get the following response:

```
{
    "_index" : "index",
    "_type" : "_doc",
    "_id" : "7OssOHIBCxugYrgStg5D",
    "_score" : 1.0,
    "_source" : {
       "product category" : "Formal shoes."
    }
}
```

This way, we can improve the search performance by fetching only the required fields instead of all the fields from the index.

Use of faster hardware

To increase the indexing performance, we can also use faster drives like SSD drives as their performance is better in comparison to the spinning disks. We should always prefer local storage instead of a remote filesystem like SMB or NFS. Virtualized storage like AWS Elastic Block Storage should also be avoided. Cloud storage is easy to set up and fast, but it is slower than dedicated local storage for the ongoing process, which is why we should use local storage. So, we can improve indexing performance using SSD drives.

Allocate memory to the filesystem cache

We can buffer the I/O operation using the filesystem cache. This can provide a performance boost because the cache can be used as a buffer. For the filesystem cache, we can assign half of the memory on the node running Elasticsearch.

Avoid including stop words in the search

We should avoid including the stop word in the query as they may explode the result count. For example, if we are searching "cow" from a document set, it will show few results matching the cow, but if we search "the cow", it will return almost all documents as this stopword "the" is quite common and can be found in all documents. Elasticsearch generates the score for a different search, and Elasticsearch has to make additional efforts if we use a stopword, which will slow down performance. If it is required to get the result for "the cow", we can use the "and" operator between "the" and "cow" to get the same match.

Avoid the script in the query

We should avoid the script as it costs more for a query. Let's take an example of a script query, where we want to search all documents with product category starting with "For" in the index. We must execute the following script query for that:

```
GET index/_search
{
  "query": {
    "bool": {
      "filter": [
        {
          "script": {
            "script": {
    "source": "doc['product category.keyword'].value.startsWith('For')
"
            }
          }
        }
      ]
    }
  }
}
```

We will get all matching documents where the product category will start with "For"; for example, refer to the following result document:

```
{
        "_index" : "index",
        "_type" : "_doc",
        "_id" : "7OssOHIBCxugYrgStg5D",
        "_score" : 0.0,
        "_source" : {
          "product category" : "Formal shoes",
          "size" : 14,
          "size_range" : "10-15"
      }
  }
```

The preceding document is an example of all those documents that will be returned after executing the script query. The issue is that the script query will require additional resources and will slow down the search query. We can use other ways to avoid the script tag, like the prefix query. Here's an example:

```
GET index/_search
{
    "query": {
        "prefix" : { "product category.keyword": "For" }
    }
}
```

Executing the preceding command can provide the same results that we get using the script query we mentioned earlier. This way, we can improve the query performance of Elasticsearch by avoiding the script queries.

These were some ways to improve the Elasticsearch search performance.

Tuning Elasticsearch for disk usage

Now that we have covered some ways to tune the indexing performance and search performance of Elasticsearch, let's explore different ways to optimize disk usage. It is important to optimize the disk usage and remove any unnecessary data from the disk, as it may eat up resources and be a bottleneck. Let's discuss some options to optimize the Elasticsearch disk usage.

Shrink index

We can reduce the shards count in an index using the shrink API. We can significantly reduce the shards count and segments of an index using this API along with the force merge API, which we will discuss in the next section. The shrink API shrinks the index and creates a new index with fewer primary shards. We must check a few things before applying the shrink API: the source index should be read-only, the copy of every shard must reside in the same node, and cluster health must be green. The following expression provides the shrink API example:

```
POST /source_index/_shrink/target_index
{
  "settings": {
    "index.number_of_replicas": 1,
    "index.number_of_shards": 1,
    "index.codec": "best_compression"
```

```
    }
}
```

Here, we are shrinking the source index into the `target_index`. This way, we can use the shrink API to shrink a read-only index and save disk utilization.

Force merge

Elasticsearch uses shards to store the index data, and each shard is a Lucene index. Shards are made up of one or more segments, and these are actual files saved on the disk. For improved efficiency, it is good to have larger segments to store the data. Using the force merge API, we can reduce the segment count by merging the segments. We can use the force merge API to merge the shards for one or more indices. Although merging happens automatically in Elasticsearch, it is better to do it manually sometimes. We should do the force merge only once the data write is completed for that index. The following command provides an example to force merge an index:

```
POST /indexname/_forcemerge
```

Here, we can force merge the index shards by applying the `_forcemerge` endpoint to the index. We can force merge all indices using the following command:

```
POST /_forcemerge
```

The preceding command will force merge all the indices. We can also force merge some indices by providing them in a comma-separated form, as shown in this example:

```
POST /indexname1, indexname2, indexname3/_forcemerge
```

This way, we can force merge the indices to save disk usage.

Disable the unrequired features

The indexing behavior of Elasticsearch allows us to index and adds doc values for almost all fields to make them available for search and aggregation. However, do we need all the fields to be indexed? Probably not. This is because we can use the values of some fields but not necessarily use them for filtering the data. So, we can disable the indexing for the fields using the following command:

```
PUT index
{
  "mappings": {
    "properties": {
```

```
      "product_code": {
        "type": "integer",
        "index": false
      }
    }
  }
}
```

In the preceding example, we are creating the mapping for the product_code field, and we are defining the index as false to instruct Elasticsearch not to index this field. Similarly, if we want to use the text field for matching but do not care about the scoring of the field, we can set the norms to false, as in this example:

```
PUT index
{
  "mappings": {
    "properties": {
      "color": {
        "type": "text",
        "norms": false
      }
    }
  }
}
```

In the preceding query, we are setting the norms as false for the color field because we don't want the score for this particular field. This way, we can tune the mapping to set only the required options and can disable the other options.

By default, Elasticsearch stores the positions for the text fields and uses that to perform the phrase queries. If we don't require the phrase queries for the field, we can disable this option using the query given here:

```
PUT index
{
  "mappings": {
    "properties": {
      "color": {
        "type": "text",
```

```
        "index_options": "freqs"
      }
    }
  }
}
```

We can use the preceding query to prevent the field from participating in the phrase query.

Avoid dynamic string mappings

By default, the Elasticsearch dynamic string mapping is applied on a string field where they are mapped as a text as well as keyword. This dual mapping is not always required and can be a waste for many fields. For example, we may not require the id field to be mapped as text and the body field as a keyword. The reason is we would never want to match the id field partially, as it should we matched exactly and has to be mapped as a keyword for that. In the case of a body field, we should match it using the text mapping where we can do a full-text search instead of an exact match. We can handle this situation by explicit mapping or by creating an index template. The following example illustrates how we can map the product id field as a keyword:

```
PUT my_index
{
  "mappings": {
    "properties": {
      "product_code": {
        "type":  "keyword"
      }
    }
  }
}
```

Here, we are mapping the `product_code` field as a keyword. The keyword is good for performing an exact match for the string field. This way, we can apply the explicit mapping to avoid dual mapping of a string field, which is wasteful in many cases.

Disable _source

The _source field in Elasticsearch response shows the actual JSON body for the document. If we do not need the document in the output, we can disable the _source field. Here's an example where we are disabling the _source field:

```
PUT index
{
  "mappings": {
    "_source": {
      "enabled": false
    }
  }
}
```

In the preceding query, we have disabled the _source field using the mapping. Now, let's add some documents to the index to understand how this change will impact the output when we search the documents. Here's an example:

```
POST index/_doc/
{
    "product category": "Formal shoes",
    "size": 5,
    "size_range": "0-5"
}
```

This example shows the creation of the document, and we can add the documents to the index using this. Now, let's search the index to return the document by executing the following command:

```
GET index/_search
```

We will get the following response:

```
 "hits" : [
     {
        "_index" : "index",
        "_type" : "_doc",
        "_id" : "ZKbrRnIBzbesIqv89MUZ",
        "_score" : 1.0
```

```
    }
]
```

There is no `_source` field in the preceding response, so we cannot see the actual document JSON but can still use the document fields for the search. So, if we do not require the document JSON on the response, we can disable it by setting the `_source` field as false in index mapping.

Use the smallest numeric type

We should use the type for numeric data that is most efficient to hold the data we want to store for the field. A data type has a significant impact on the disk usage, so it is necessary to use the type that is sufficient to store the data instead of wasting the space by mapping with a type having more size than we are planning to save. For example, integers should be saved using integer types like byte, short, integer, or long, while a floating-point value can be saved using the float, double, or `half_float`. We should know whether a float type is sufficient or a `double` type is required for storing our data. This way, we can decide the suitable type and save the disk usage.

Till now, we discussed different ways to improve indexing and search performances, and we also explored ways to optimize disk utilization. Now, we will discuss some best practices that we should follow to get the optimal results using Elasticsearch.

Elasticsearch best practices

We should follow certain best practices to optimize Elasticsearch performance and prevent any future issues. Here, we will discuss some Elasticsearch best practices.

Always define the mapping

It is a best practice to define the mapping for the Elasticsearch index before adding the documents. Before pushing the JSON data into Elasticsearch, it is always better to understand the data we want to push and its structure. Once that information is handy, we can create the mapping and then start pushing the data. The reason behind this approach is to save ourselves from any data type-related issues because Elasticsearch guesses the data type if we avoid explicit mapping, and that can sometimes be wrong. We have also covered some performance tuning options that are only possible if we follow explicit mapping for the Elasticsearch index. So, it is always advisable to explicitly create the Elasticsearch mapping for the document fields.

Do your capacity planning

We should plan for the capacity in terms of disk, memory, or CPU utilization. We must consider different aspects for the capacity planning, like what would be the data retention period, what would be the data index rate, and the data search rate. We should also consider the required number of replicas. Capacity planning takes a lot of effort, and it cannot be perfected in a single go, so we have to make improvements by refining after some benchmarking. Elasticsearch is scalable, so we have the option to scale horizontally whenever we need more capacity. In any case, initial planning is always required to make a stable cluster that can serve user requests without any issues.

Avoid split-brain problem

Elasticsearch has distributed architecture, which means a single cluster can be spread to multiple nodes (means machines). If we enable the replica shards, data can be distributed to multiple nodes, and there would not be any data loss in case of a single node failure. This distributed nature of Elasticsearch provides us with performance and high availability. Now, let's understand the split-brain issue. It is a condition that can occur if the cluster splits up because of any reason, for example, connectivity failure. In this situation, the slave nodes cannot communicate to the master node, and they assume that the master node is down. This process initiates the master node election among the connected nodes, and the new master node takes charge after the election.

On connectivity restore, we can have two master nodes. In this situation, the previous master assumes that the disconnected node will join back as a slave, while the new master node assumes that the original master node is down and will rejoin as a slave node. This situation is known as a split-brain. We can solve this issue by configuring the `discovery.zen.minimum_master_nodes` Elasticsearch parameter. We can set this parameter to half the number of nodes + 1 so that we would always require a sufficient number of nodes to elect the master node. So, we can avoid the split-brain problem.

Enable the slow query log

We can keep an eye on query performance and get the log in case the query is slow by enabling the slow query log. We can provide the duration of the query execution and the log will accordingly pick the queries where the query execution time is greater than the threshold value that we can set. After receiving the slow queries log, we can work on them to optimize their performance. We need to execute the following command to enable the slow query log:

```
PUT /index_name/_settings
```

```
{
    "index.search.slowlog.threshold.query.warn": "10s",
    "index.search.slowlog.threshold.query.info": "5s",
    "index.search.slowlog.threshold.query.debug": "2s",
    "index.search.slowlog.threshold.query.trace": "500ms",
    "index.search.slowlog.threshold.fetch.warn": "1s",
    "index.search.slowlog.threshold.fetch.info": "800ms",
    "index.search.slowlog.threshold.fetch.debug": "500ms",
    "index.search.slowlog.threshold.fetch.trace": "200ms",
    "index.search.slowlog.level": "info"
}
```

In the preceding query, we are setting various thresholds to log the slow queries. Here, we can see that the threshold value is set as 10 seconds for a warning, 5 seconds for info, and 2 seconds for debug. This way, we can configure the threshold values for the index. We will get the following response after successfully executing the preceding query:

```
{
    "acknowledged" : true
}
```

The preceding response shows that our slow query log configuration query was successful, and we can now see the slow queries in the log file. Slow query logs are useful for improving the Elasticsearch performance.

These were some best practices that we should follow to derive the optimal performance output from Elasticsearch.

Conclusion

In this chapter, we looked at how to improve Elasticsearch cluster performance. We started with tuning the indexing speed of Elasticsearch and covered various options to tune the indexing performance, like bulk requests, smart use of cluster, increasing the refresh interval, disabling replicas, using auto-generated ids, faster hardware, and increasing the filesystem cache. Then, we explored different options to tune the search speed, like document modelling, search a few fields, pre-index data, filter instead of query, and increase the replica count. We also covered various ways to improve disk usage, like shrink index, force merge, avoid dynamic string mapping, and many other options. Finally, we went over some best practices to derive better performance from an Elasticsearch cluster.

In the next chapter, we will understand how to administer the Elasticsearch cluster. We will cover different topics, like how to apply security on the Elasticsearch cluster, how to create index aliases, and how to take a snapshot and restore it. We will also cover the Elastic Common Schema.

Questions

1. How can we tune the Elasticsearch indexing speed?

2. What is the refresh interval in Elasticsearch?

3. How can we tune the search speed of Elasticsearch?

4. Differentiate filter and query in Elasticsearch.

5. How can we fetch only the required fields in Elasticsearch?

6. How can we tune the disk usage in Elasticsearch?

CHAPTER 11
Administering Elasticsearch

In the last chapter, we looked at how to improve Elasticsearch cluster performance. We started with tuning the indexing speed of Elasticsearch and then explored different options to tune the search performance of an Elasticsearch cluster. We also covered various ways to improve the disk usage of an Elasticsearch cluster. At last, we covered some best practices to enhance the performance of an Elasticsearch cluster. In this chapter, we will discuss how we can perform some administrative tasks in Elasticsearch. We will start with security and explain how to apply the security in Elasticsearch. Then, we will understand how to create the index aliases and what is snapshot and restore in terms of Elasticsearch. After that, we will learn how to take snapshots of Elasticsearch indices and how to restore them. At the end, we will look at the Elastic Common Schema and understand its importance.

Structure

In this chapter, we will cover the following:

- Elasticsearch security
- Index aliases
- Creating repository and snapshot
- Restoring a snapshot
- Elastic common schema

Objectives

After studying this unit, you should be able to:

- Configure the Elasticsearch security
- Configure the index aliases
- Take snapshot and restore it

Elasticsearch security

From Elastic Stack 6.8 and 7.1 onwards, many Elasticsearch security features are available for free. These include features like TLS encryption for communication and **role-based access control (RBAC).** Here, we will understand how you can configure the TLS and authentication, and then we will look at how we can connect Kibana securely with Elasticsearch. Here, I am assuming that Elasticsearch and Kibana are already installed on your machine. Installing Kibana is not mandatory here, but you would be able to test how we can configure the role-based access control using the Kibana interface if it is installed. The Kibana interface provides us with an interface to create roles and users, and we can assign the roles to different users. Now, let's see how we can configure the TLS on Elasticsearch cluster. This example has a single node of the cluster, but we can copy the same configuration to different nodes in case of multiple nodes.

Configuring TLS

For TLS configuration, we must first generate the certificates, using which the nodes will communicate securely. We can get the certificates from an enterprise CA, which is the right way to configure the TLS, but let's see how you can configure TLS without taking the certificates from any CA. Elasticsearch provides us a `elasticsearch-certutil` command, using which we can configure TLS without the usual certificates. We have to follow these steps to configure the TLS:

1. Move to the Elasticsearch home location; for example, we can execute the following command on Ubuntu:

   ```
   cd /usr/share/elasticsearch/
   ```

2. Now, execute the following `elasticsearch-certutil` command:

   ```
   bin/elasticsearch-certutil cert -out config/elastic-certificates.
   p12 -pass ""
   ```

3. We will get the following response:

   Certificates written to /usr/share/elasticsearch/config/elastic-certificates.p12

This file should be properly secured as it contains the private key for your instance.

This file is a self contained file and can be copied and used 'as is' For each Elastic product that you wish to configure, you should copy this '.p12' file to the relevant configuration directory and then follow the SSL configuration instructions in the product guide.

4. After getting the success, open the `elasticsearch.yml` file from etc/ elasticsearch/ and copy the following lines:

   `xpack.security.enabled: true`

   `xpack.security.transport.ssl.enabled: true`

   `xpack.security.transport.ssl.verification_mode: certificate`

   `xpack.security.transport.ssl.keystore.path: elastic-certificates. p12`

   `xpack.security.transport.ssl.truststore.path: elastic-certificates.p12`

5. Then, we need to save the file and start the Elasticsearch service:

   `sudo service elasticsearch start`

We can start the Elasticsearch service using the preceding command.

Elasticsearch cluster passwords

After starting the Elasticsearch service, we can configure the password for the Elasticsearch cluster by following these steps:

1. Move to the Elasticsearch Home directory and execute the following command:

   `bin/elasticsearch-setup-passwords auto`

2. After executing the preceding command, Elasticsearch will ask for confirmation before setting the passwords for different in-built users like `apm_system`, `kibana`, `logstash_system`, `beats_system`, `remote_ monitoring_user`, and elastic user. We will get the following response after executing the preceding command:

   Initiating the setup of passwords for reserved users elastic,apm_ system,kibana,logstash_system,beats_system,remote_ monitoring_user.

   The passwords will be randomly generated and printed to the console.

   Please confirm that you would like to continue [y/N]y

```
Changed password for user apm_system
PASSWORD apm_system = ITWroWSyMRlDHDYpzQdP

Changed password for user kibana
PASSWORD kibana = aiX6OBRdlJdgXU4faCyK

Changed password for user logstash_system
PASSWORD logstash_system = wNAbnUNSy8bMs09vhH62

Changed password for user beats_system
PASSWORD beats_system = Tmo7y8MjxN93XAPrkc0S

Changed password for user remote_monitoring_user
PASSWORD remote_monitoring_user = gNkO8z6UhZtkVmzkn922

Changed password for user elastic
PASSWORD elastic = fPl2L4sieawIcaWMxSUE
```

3. This way, we can create automatic passwords for in-built users. If we want to manually set the passwords, we can remove the auto part from the command.

4. The security is now enabled in Elasticsearch, and we can confirm this by executing this command:

    curl localhost:9200

5. We will get the following response:

```
{
  "error" : {
    "root_cause" : [
      {
        "type" : "security_exception",
        "reason" : "missing authentication credentials for REST
request [/?pretty]",
        "header" : {
          "WWW-Authenticate" : "Basic realm=\"security\"
charset=\"UTF-8\""
        }
      }
    ],
```

```
    "type" : "security_exception",

    "reason" : "missing authentication credentials for REST
request [/?pretty]",

    "header" : {

        "WWW-Authenticate" : "Basic realm=\"security\"
charset=\"UTF-8\""

    }

  },

  "status" : 401

}
```

6. Now, if we want to access Elasticsearch, we have to pass the username and password as well. Refer to the following command:

   curl elastic:fPl2L4sieawIcaWMxSUE@localhost:9200

7. In the preceding command, we are passing the username as elastic and password as fPl2L4sieawIcaWMxSUE, along with the curl request. We will get the following output after executing the preceding command:

```
{

  "name" : "anurag-HP-EliteBook-840-G1",

  "cluster_name" : "elasticsearch",

  "cluster_uuid" : "ifQu5sObR4S7PwL0y2yfzg",

  "version" : {

    "number" : "7.6.2",

    "build_flavor" : "default",

    "build_type" : "deb",

    "build_hash" : "ef48eb35cf30adf4db14086e8aabd07ef6fb113f",

    "build_date" : "2020-03-26T06:34:37.794943Z",

    "build_snapshot" : false,

    "lucene_version" : "8.4.0",

     "minimum_wire_compatibility_version" : "6.8.0",

    "minimum_index_compatibility_version" : "6.0.0-beta1"

  },

  "tagline" : "You Know, for Search"

}
```

8. This way, we can configure the security in Elasticsearch.

After configuring the security in Elasticsearch, we have to configure Kibana so that it can work. If we try to run Kibana without making any changes, we will get the following message:

```
Kibana server is not ready yet
```

So, let's configure Kibana with Elasticsearch username and password by updating the `kibana.yml` file located under `/etc/kibana/` on Ubuntu. After opening the `kibana.yml` file, we must uncomment the username and password and configure the newly created password. Refer to the following snippet of the `kibana.yml` file:

```
elasticsearch.username: "kibana"
elasticsearch.password: "aiX6OBRdlJdgXU4faCyK"
```

After modifying the Elasticsearch username and password, we need to restart Kibana using the command given here:

```
sudo service kibana restart
```

On the Kibana URL **http://localhost:5601**, we can get the login screen. Take a look at the following screenshot:

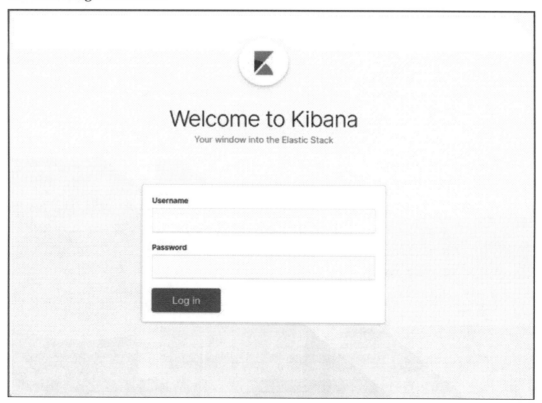

Figure 11.1: Kibana login screen

Now, we can use the username and password we created using the Elasticsearch tool to log in to Kibana.

Configuring role-based access using Kibana

Now, we will understand how to configure different roles, users, and how we can assign the roles to the users using the Kibana interface. Let's first look at how we can create the users.

Creating users

Let's see how to create different users, as it is required when you want to give Kibana access to different users. We can restrict the access of different indices and other components to different users based on their roles, which we will cover next. We need to do the following to create users in Kibana:

1. After logging in to Kibana, click on the **Management** link from the left menu to open the Management screen of Kibana.

2. Then, click on the **Users** link under the **Security** option.

    This will open the **Users** screen with a list of the existing, pre-defined users of Elasticsearch, like `elastic`, `kibana`, `logstash_system`, `beats_system`, and such. Refer to the following screenshot:

Figure 11.2: Kibana user listing

3. To create a new user, click on the **Create user** button on top-right corner.

4. We get a new user registration form where we can add the username, password, full name, email address, and such, and we can assign one or many roles. Take a look at the following screenshot:

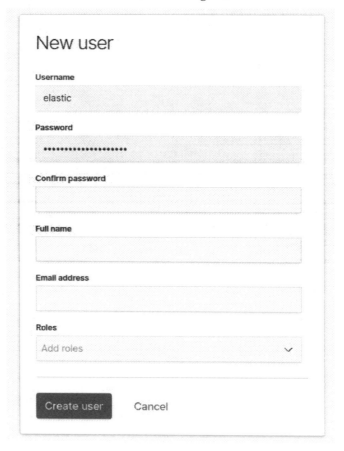

Figure 11.3: Kibana user creation screen

5. After filling the form, click on the **Create user** button to create the user. This will again open the user listing page, where we can see our newly created user.

   We can edit a custom user by clicking on the username link on the user listing screen.

   We can delete a user by clicking on the user's checkbox and then on the **Delete user** button. We can also delete the user from the edit screen by clicking on the delete user button.

This way, we can create users from the Kibana Management page. Now, let's understand how to create the roles.

Creating roles

We can create different users and assign different roles to them. The roles can have different permissions, using which we can restrict users' access, like access to selected indices of Elasticsearch. To create the roles, we need to do the following:

1. After logging in to Kibana, click on the **Management** link from the left menu to open the Management screen of Kibana.

2. Then, click on the **Roles** link under the **Security** option. This will open the roles listing page with all the existing pre-defined roles. The following screenshot illustrates this:

Figure 11.4: Kibana role listing screen

3. The preceding screenshot shows the listing of pre-defined roles. We need to click on the **Click role** button in the top-right corner to create a new role.

4. This will open the **Create role** page where we can configure the role name, role settings like cluster privileges, run as privileges, and index privileges.

We can also configure the Kibana access privileges. Refer to the following screenshot:

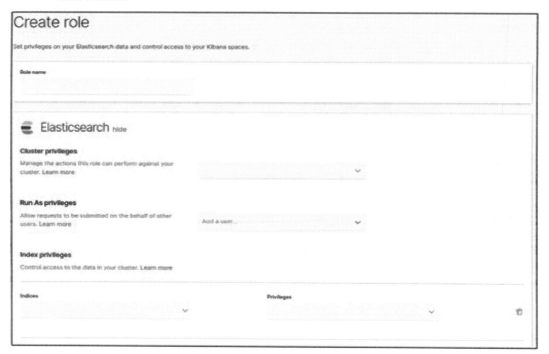

Figure 11.5: Kibana role creation screen

5. After configuring the role permissions, we can click on the **Create role** button to save the role. From the user listing page, we can edit the user and assign roles to the user.

Index aliases

The aliases in Elasticsearch provide us with a way to refer the index with a secondary name. Here, we map the index with an alias name and use it to execute different queries on the index. We can also map more than one index with the same alias name. You may be wondering why you should create an alias for the index. It's because it is helpful in many ways, like if you want to reindex without the downtime or club multiple index data to monitor them. Now, let's see how we can create an alias on an index using the following example:

```
POST /_aliases
{
    "actions" : [
        { "add" : { "index" : "userdetails", "alias" : "users_alias" } }
```

```
        ]
}
```

Here, we are creating the `users_alias` alias using the `userdetails` index. To create or remove the aliases, we have to use the `_aliases` endpoint. Once the alias is created, we can remove the index alias using the following expression:

```
POST /_aliases
{
    "actions" : [
        { "remove" : { "index" : "userdetails", "alias" : "users_alias"
} }
    ]
}
```

In the preceding expression, we are removing the `users_alias` alias from the `userdetails` index. This way, we can add or remove the aliases from one or more indices. If we want to add more than one index for a single alias name, we can execute the expression given here:

```
POST /_aliases
{
    "actions" : [
        { "add" : { "indices" : ["userdetails", "user_details"], "alias"
: "users_alias" } }
    ]
}
```

This way, a single alias name can show the combined results of more than one index. Now, let's discuss how we can enable zero downtime reindexing using index aliases. We can enable a zero downtime reindexing in Elasticsearch using the index aliases. Sometimes, we need to reindex an Elasticsearch index, for example, to change the mapping of some fields. Let's assume that we have index1, using which we are serving an application, and now we want to `reindex` it to `index2`. So, we must change the index mapping of the application once the reindexing is done, but we can save this as follows using aliases:

- Let's assume that we have `index1` that we want to reindex to `index2`.

- In the first step, we should create an alias and map it to index1.

- The purpose of this alias is to remove the dependency from the `index1` name.

- In the next step, map the application with alias name instead of the `index1` name.

- Then, reindex `index1` to `index2` and remove the alias mapping with index1 and map it with `index2` once the process is complete. This can be done using a single command, as shown here:

```
POST /_aliases
{
    "actions" : [
          { "remove" : { "indices" : "index1", "alias" : "users_
alias" } },
          { "add" : { "indices" : "index2", "alias" : "users_alias"
} }
    ]
}
```

- In the preceding expression, we are removing the alias mapping from `index1` and mapping it with `index2`. This way, we can perform the reindexing without making any change to the running application.

Repository and snapshot

Snapshot is the backup of the Elasticsearch cluster that can be restored to retrieve the data in case of any failure. We can take the snapshot of the complete cluster or individual indices of Elasticsearch and store these snapshots on a local machine or remote locations like S3 bucket, Google cloud storage, or Azure cloud. The snapshot takes incremental backup, where each new snapshot contains data after the last snapshot. Using the restore API, we can restore the Elasticsearch snapshot. We can restore the complete snapshot of only a few indices, and we can also change the name and settings of the index during restore. However, we need to register the repository before taking the snapshot. So, let's see how we can create the repository on the local storage; let's take the example of a local machine for snapshot and restore.

Creating the repository

So, we first need to create a repository before taking the snapshot, and we should keep a separate repository for each cluster. Using the repository API, we can create the repository on the local machine but we must first specify the directory location where we want to store the snapshot files. We need to do the following to create a repository:

1. Identify the directory location to store the snapshot; here, I am taking an example as `/var/tmp/backups`, but we can create the backups directory anywhere with any name.

2. Once the directory is created, we need to give it the required permissions so that Elasticsearch can write the snapshot to this location. We can provide the owner permission to Elasticsearch using the following command:

   chown -R elasticsearch. /var/tmp/backups

3. Once the permission is given to the backup directory, we need to add this path to the `repo.path` settings of the Elasticsearch configuration file. So, open the `elasticsearch.yml` file and add the following:

   path.repo: ["/var/tmp/backups"]

4. We have configured path.repo, so we can now create the repository using which we can take the snapshot and restore it. Execute the following command to create the repository:

```
PUT _snapshot/anurag_backup
{
  "type": "fs",
  "settings": {
    "location": "/var/tmp/backups"
  }
}
```

We can unregister the repository using the command given as follows:

DELETE _snapshot/anurag_backup

If we want to see the details of all the repositoritories, we can use the following command:

GET /_snapshot/_all

The preceding command lists down all available repositories. Our `anurag_backup` repository is created, so we can now take the snapshot.

Taking the snapshot

Our repository is ready, so let's take the snapshot of some indices to understand how this snapshot and restore works. We have already discussed that a snapshot can have all indices of a cluster or can have one or more indices. If we want to take the snapshot of all indices of the cluster, we can execute the following command:

PUT _snapshot/anurag_backup/snapshot_all_indices

The preceding command will start the backup in the given snapshot name by giving immediate response. However, if we want to ensure the snapshot creation after executing the command, we can add flag `wait_for_completion` with the command. This will enable Elasticsearch to wait for the response till the snapshot is completed. Refer to the following command:

```
PUT _snapshot/anurag_backup/snapshot_all_indices?wait_for_
completion=true
```

If we want to take a snapshot of a few indices instead of all, we can specify the index names is a comma-separated way against the indices key of the command. This enables us to take the snapshot only for the specified indices. Refer to the following command:

```
PUT _snapshot/anurag_backup/snapshot_few_indices
{
 "indices": "index1, index2"
}
```

This way, we can create the snapshot for one or more indices. We can see the details of a snapshot using the following command:

```
GET /_snapshot/anurag_backup/snapshot_few_indices
```

This shows the details for the `snapshot_few_indices` snapshot, where we have used `index1` and `index2` to create the snapshot. If we want to see all snapshots of the repository, we can execute the following command:

```
GET /_snapshot/anurag_backup/_all
```

The preceding command can be used to list down all snapshots of the `anurag_backup` repository. We can also list all snapshot among all the available repositories using the following command:

```
GET /_snapshot/_all
```

We have not mentioned the repository name in the preceding query, so it will find and list the snapshot on all available repositories. If we want to see the current running snapshot that is not yet complete, we can execute the following command:

```
GET /_snapshot/anurag_backup/_current
```

This way, we can create the snapshot for one or more indices. We can delete the snapshot using the following command:

```
DELETE /_snapshot/anurag_backup/snapshot_few_indices
```

The preceding command will delete the `snapshot_few_indices` snapshot. So, using the above-mentioned snapshot APIs, we can create, view, or delete the snapshot. Till now, we have covered how to create the repository and take the snapshot. Now, let's see how we can restore the snapshot in Elasticsearch.

Restoring a snapshot

We can restore the snapshot using the `_restore` endpoint. By default, the restore process restores all the indices of the snapshot, but we can also select the indices we want to restore. The restore process is very simple, and we just need to add the `_restore` endpoint in the API. Refer to the following example:

```
POST /_snapshot/my_backup/snapshot_name/_restore
```

We can perform the restore process on any functional cluster of Elasticsearch. If we are trying to restore an index that is already active in the cluster, we need to close it. Also, the number of shards has to be the same. If the index is available and closed, the Elasticsearch restore process will open the index, and it will create the index if it is not there. If we want to restore some indices from the snapshot, we can do that using the following query:

```
POST /_snapshot/my_backup/snapshot_name/_restore
{
  "indices": "index1,index2",
  "ignore_unavailable": true,
  "include_aliases": false,
  "include_global_state": false
}
```

In this example, we are restoring `index1` and `index2`. There are many other options, like `include_aliases`, using which we can include the aliases as well. Using `include_global_state`, we can restore the snapshot's cluster state, but it is false by default. The global state restores the index templates, ingest pipelines, persistent settings, and such. This way, we can create the snapshot of an Elasticsearch cluster for one or more indices and restore it to an active cluster.

Elastic common schema

Elastic Common Schema is a specification that ensures consistency in the structure of Elasticsearch data. ECS provides us a way to easily remember the field names, as it supports similar common names for the fields instead of different names for a similar type of field. It helps us uniformly examine the data, enabling better data analysis and visualizations, and such.

Why do we need a common schema?

In normal cases, we ingest data from different sources. There may be common fields but the name of those fields may not be common. For example, an IP field can be different for a log file, metrics data, and APM data. In that case, we need to handle all of them; let's say we want to query a particular IP address, so we have to write multiple queries and join them with OR condition. We are facing these issues because we pulled data from different sources, and they all have different sets of standards.

During analysis, search, or visualization, we have to find all field names representing a similar entity like IP address or username. Once that is identified, we can perform these operations; so, it is an additional overhead where we first need to understand the data and then do the analysis. Here, the Elastic Common Schema is very useful and required, as it can result in a common field name among different data sources. Also, it reduces the additional overhead of field mapping because the same field name is used for a different data source.

Introduction to Elastic common schema

As we already discussed, Elastic Common Schema is an open-source specification to define the fields of different documents in a common set. We ingest data from different sources, and they may have different common fields with different names. Here, Elastic Common Schema helps us by providing a uniform name for common fields, using which we can easily work on a different set of data without understanding how the data is associated with a field for the source. The Elastic Common Schema enables us to ingest data from different sources and analyze it centrally. This is possible because ECS supports uniform data modelling, and we can access the IP address fields using the IP field name instead of `remote_ip, user. ip,` or `src_ip`.

The Elastic Common Schema organizes the data elements in three levels based on their taxonomy:

- **ECS Core Fields:** ECS core fields are fields that are common for different use cases. Using these fields, we can do the data analysis, search, visualization, and such. The ECS core fields are fully defined in Elasticsearch.

- **ECS Extended Fields:** After the core fields, we have extended ECS fields. They are not fully defined as they have partially defined a set of field names. The ECS extended fields also come under top-level objects set of ECS.

- **Custom fields:** The fields that are not defined under ECS specifications are known as custom fields. These fields are the user-defined fields and have no conflict with the ECS fields.

ECS general guidelines

There are some general guidelines to be considered for the Elastic Common Schema:

- Each document must have a `@timestamp` field.
- We should use the ECS defined data types.
- We should include the `ecs.version` field to define the ECS version we are using.
- We should map the maximum possible fields to ECS.

ECS field name guidelines

Apart from the general guidelines for the ECS, there are some guidelines for the field names for the ECS specifications. Now, let's discuss those field name guidelines for ECS:

- The field names must be in lower case.
- We should combine the words through the underscore sign.
- There is no support for special characters, except underscore.
- We should nest the fields as a fieldset using dots.
- The nesting of fieldset goes from general to specific; for example, `host.ip`.
- We should avoid any repetition, like `host.host_ip` should be written as `host.ip`.
- We should avoid abbreviations if possible.
- We should use the present tense for the field names unless it is showing historical information.
- We should use the singular or plural names as per the requirement, like the type of data it is referring to.

Getting started with ECS

If we are using the latest Beats for data ingestion, we are already using the Elastic Common Schema as Beats has already implemented the ECS specifications. If we are ingesting data from a source using Logstash, we can tweak it as per the ECS specification so that we can work on different sets of data centrally without any issue. We can confirm that the document has ECS formatting by referring to the `ecs.version` field name as it shows the version number for the ECS. Refer to the following Apache log as an example:

127.0.0.1 - - [07/Jun/2020:11:05:07 +0100] "GET /user HTTP/1.1" 200 2571 "-" "Mozilla/5.0 (Macintosh; Intel Mac OS X 10_14_0) AppleWebKit/537.36 (KHTML, like Gecko) Chrome/70.0.3538.102 Safari/537.36"

Now see below the field names it contains as per ECS:

@timestamp

ecs.version

event.dataset

event.original

http.request.method

http.request.body.bytes

http.response.status_code

http.version

host.hostname

message

service.name

service.type

service.geo.*

source.ip

url.original

user.name

user.agent.*

The preceding field names are defined as per the ECS specifications, and we can also see the `ecs.version` field that holds the ECS version number. I have already mentioned that ECS can help us simplify things, whether search, analysis, or visualization. For example, if we have to search the IP without ECS, the search query can be as follows:

src:127.0.0.1 OR client_ip:127.0.0.1 OR apache2.access.remote_
ip:127.0.0.1 OR context.user.ip:127.0.0.1 OR src_ip:127.0.0.1

If we are using the ECS, the same query can be simplified as shown:

source.ip: 127.0.0.1

Similarly, it will also simplify all other operations that we may perform using the data. So, it is important to use the ECS specification whenever we are ingesting data from any source to Elasticsearch.

Conclusion

In this chapter, we discussed how to administer the Elasticsearch cluster. We also covered different topics, like how to apply security on the Elasticsearch cluster, how to create the index aliases, and how to take a snapshot and restore it. We also explored the Elastic Common Schema.

Questions

1. How can we secure the Elasticsearch cluster?

2. How can we create the index alias in Elasticsearch?

3. How can we create the repository in Elasticsearch?

4. How can we take the snapshot in Elasticsearch, and how can we restore it?

5. What is Elastic common schema?

Index

Made in the USA
Middletown, DE
24 September 2023